PSYCHOLOGY, NORMAL AND ABNORMAL

PSYCHOLOGY, NORMAL AND ABNORMAL

A STUDY OF THE PROCESSES OF NATURE FROM THE INNER ASPECT

WARREN E. LLOYD

GYAN

Published by

Gyan Publishing House
5, Ansari Road
Daryaganj, New Delhi-110002
Phone: 011-47034999, 9811692060
E-mail: books@gyanbooks.com

Distribution Network
gyanbooks.com
India, USA, Canada, UK, Australia

ISBN: 978-93-7169-428-5 (PB)

First Published, 1908

2nd Impression 2025

Printed at: Gyan Press, Delhi.

PSYCHOLOGY, NORMAL AND ABNORMAL
Author: WARREN E. LLOYD

PSYCHOLOGY, NORMAL AND ABNORMAL

PSYCHOLOGY, NORMAL AND ABNORMAL

A STUDY OF THE PROCESSES OF NATURE
FROM THE INNER ASPECT

BY
WARREN E. LLOYD, M. L., PH. D.
ASSISTED BY
ANNIE ELIZABETH CHENEY

BAUMGARDT PUBLISHING CO.
LOS ANGELES, CAL.

CRITIQUE.

There will be many critiques written on this book, but we are bound to write the first; afterward the world may say what it will.

This text book is based on a first principle and logically reasoned out. Were its foundation good and structure bad, it would be like a house of wood on a base of stone—easily burned by fire. Were its foundation bad and its structure good, it would be like a granite fort standing on wooden piles—sure sooner or later to fall by its own weight.

Now whatever the learned may say hereafter (and the learned will most surely investigate this book), they cannot undermine its foundation or destroy its structure. Call this foundation (principle) an hypothesis, if you choose, even a Spencer could never disprove it. Should some sage of the Twentieth Century declare that **polarity** is not a first principle, we would most sincerely ask him if by first he means precedence as regards others, or if by first he means the most important. Whichever he means, even though will (desire) may possibly be the cause of causes, we defy him to show how polarity can be wrenched from that same primeval sovereign will when it projects itself into objectivity; more, we defy him to detach that same almighty will from objectivity. Therefore, for all psychology, for all practice in living, for all experiment in activities in time and space, polarity **is** the first principle, and no doctor in philosophy can prove it otherwise. Being then on a foundation unassailable, the base upon which this book is built is assured. As to the structure, the authors having justified themselves as to the two methods of dealing with energy; first as constant, second as apparently transferable; no flaw can be found in the logic from start to finish. In fact, it is **unusual** in that it

emphasizes the mathematics of energy as probably no text book on psychology has done before.

This book is written for thinkers and students in the problems of life's riddle. It throws no sop to the Cerberus of superstition, it pampers no morbid dabbler in so-called "new thought," it tickles no nerve of religious fanaticism; but straightforwardly relies upon principle, logic and facts, daringly throwing down the gauntlet to antiquated psychology, and through its up-to-dateness in all directions defies bigotry and challenges criticism.

It is a text book for students in colleges and a volume for their professors also. The time has come when the inherent truths of the various sciences and philosophies must be marshalled and related into a psychology that shall have no weak point, but shall be found logical from its interior as well as its exterior aspect. Of late the world of psychology, except where using physical methods, has satisfied itself with works on economics, ethics and sociology, ignoring to a great extent the splendid a priori inner world which flowers the instant it touches objectivity. Brain cells and the cortex of the cerebum are very well as far as they go, but memory and imagination are beyond and above them and demand a solution in principle as well as in matter.

It is safe to say that a profound study of this work will have a practical outcome, and we dare to assert that he who delves into it deeply enough will find a key to the problem of life itself.

Little attempt has been made in this text book to deal with data newly discovered, or facts gained by specialists along any of the lines of modern research that might bear on the question, for, once having started in the trails of these sleuths of modern sciences, there would be no end to the fruit gleaned and no possible way in the limited space of a compact work of this kind of dealing with it satisfactorily.

So the effort rests contentedly on its principle alone, leaving the world at large to apply it in every conceivable way to every possible new datum discoverable, knowing that to the pendulum accuracy of the rhythm of polarity all data must inevitably be subject. The Law of Antithesis is a yardstick divided into inches, and no century to come can produce data that it may not measure. Comparative psychology is now so much in vogue, the researchers along that line inquisitively hunting facts, discarding no specimen whether it be a learned dog, a mathematical horse or a deaf and dumb prodigy, that it seems like reviving the days of Hegel when a Doctor of Philosophy comes forth and makes a stand for a **principle** as the solvent and explanation of every datum possible. He reverses modern processes and is dynamic rather than inductive. "The explosive is here," he says. "Bring on your facts and I can blow them into ultimate condition by this never failing law."

The principle is not new nor mysterious. We contend only that it is seldom applied, grasped or understood. Modern psychologists ignore it and lose their balance in their emphasis of effects, forgetting that married to them is their cause as clearly defined as the sun in heaven. But this same sun blinds the specialists' eyes, and spectacled they grope enthusiastically for data as though there could ever be a finish and an end to the procession of the infinite.

CONTENTS

CHAPTER V.

Pleasure and Pain.

CHAPTER VI.

Imagery.

CHAPTER VII.

Memory and Imagination.

CHAPTER VIII.

Intuition and Understanding.

CHAPTER IX.

Periodicity.

CHAPTER X.

Poise.

INTRODUCTION.

1. The Necessity for a Hypothesis.

The use of assumptions and hypotheses as instruments of investigation in the sciences being universal, we can see no reason why psychology should attempt to avoid this method. Her failure to make proper advance seems to arise from weakness in this line. The old psychology had the assumption of a mind or of a soul whose faculties and experiences constituted mental life. Whether tenable or not, this hypothesis gave definiteness to the matters treated and made them comprehensible, so that our ordinary ideas regarding mind and mental processes to this day are couched in its terms.

Under the influence of modern science a reaction against speculative teachings and doctrines led to a discarding of the old hypothesis, but so far psychology does not seem to have found a satisfactory new one. Physiological psychology and psycho-physics, while diligent and patient in their methods, can hardly claim to be more than specializations of nerve physiology and cerebral anatomy. They have no means of going beyond the territory illuminated by their physical methods of search. On the other hand, most of those who revel in abnormal and occult phenomena travel in that obscure realm without hypothesis, chart, or compass. Their journeys are erratic and the wares they bring home hardly worth considering.

But the subject is far too vital to be avoided. The natural sciences are piling up material facts and noting laws in which we begin to lose interest because of the uncertain attitude of science toward the invisible side of life. The realm of psychology must be conquered or modern civilization itself is imperiled.

With a proper hypothesis, the facts of mental life will be explained and investigated with the same facility as in the physical realm. Also the knowledge gained will have as practical a bearing as that which has given such impetus to material progress. While the need of a better understanding of the nature of thought and mental processes is pressing, and inspires these pages, the application of the principles to be enunciated is not within the scope of this book. A true and proper analysis of psychological problems is our aim, and, if attained, practice can be left to take care of itself.

By abnormal, we mean only that which is unclassified and unusual. Some nexus or relation to the normal must be discovered; for psychology can no more tolerate uncaused phenomena than can her law-abiding sisters of natural science. The matter as far as investigated must be made intelligible, even if the structure is left incomplete. All principles and laws discovered by science are only portions of the larger house of knowledge. The beams and structural parts thus discerned will be given final architectural shape by philosophy.

If, in this investigation, we shall advance a hypothesis which explains the known facts of mental life and leads to the discovery of the principles governing the more obscure and subtle processes of inner nature, it can be accepted as the true basis of our present individual life and a stable part of the foundation in which all things have their eternal existence.

2. Physiological Psychology as a Natural Science.

Proceeding with the analysis of the problem, let us define the field in which psychology must work. It is the aim of the natural sciences to explain nature. In one sense they claim that nature includes everything, yet, while so doing, they confine themselves to a particular conception of matter and to investigating the physical forces affecting it. This attitude is common to all the natural sciences. Their laws establish only the modes of motion of matter and the properties manifested by it.

For this reason, they are all interdependent. Starting with the earth as the unit, geology studies its history since its formation and shows the progressive modification of the earth's crust. Astronomy pushes the history further back and takes up the question of its relation to the heavenly bodies. Spectroscopy and stellar photography work out more details of constitution and structure. Going forward, chemistry and physics begin their qualitative work. Botany, zoology and kindred sciences treat of organic life, and anthropology in its widest significance includes all human activities.

In this series, physiological psychology could begin only with sentient life. It would be the science dealing with the sensations and conscious processes of living organisms arising from or correlated with the motions of the matter of which they are composed.

Under this conception it is inevitable that psychology be assigned a secondary place. Sentiency and consciousness, as thus understood, are not very pervasive. The first tendency is to confine them to cerebral matter and organized brains. If an extension is made to ganglionic centers and neural matter in general, it is with an implied understanding that the search should stop there. Only nerve cells are supposed to feel.

In spite of this positiveness, there is dissatisfaction with the situation. Nature abhors a vacuum and discontinuity. By the hypothesis of other sciences, all organic structures arise by the continuous process of evolution. If this is true, nerve cells and brains are similarly created. The point then at which sensation ought to arise cannot be determined. A worse difficulty is got into by treating it as a wholly dissimilar product after it has arisen. We shall not elaborate these points here. It is certain, that if consciousness comes from the motions of nerve and brain cells, it must be implied in the motion of all the constituent atoms and molecules which compose those cells. These molecules, however, come from and return to other forms of matter. Therefore it was said that the consciousness of the organism arises from the motion of the matter of which it is composed.

3. The Problem of Knowledge.

There is one point of view from which psychology cannot be treated as a science with a limited conception of consciousness. This arises from a consideration of the fact that all knowledge of external nature comes to us from sensations and mental imagery. In order to hang these phenomena together, we have the ideas of substance, time, space and causality. Whether these ideas come from external nature or internal mind, we cannot say. From the point of view of knowledge, the mental half of the transaction is as important as the material world in which sensation is supposed to have its origin.

It appears, then, that the knowing subject stands over against the perceived object in strict and complete opposition. Nature cannot be understood or enlarged without the knower expanding likewise. If nature is conceived as a fixed and determinable quantity, the person or being who can perceive or understand nature must be in relation to nature in all its parts. If subject and object are not in relation, each is non-existent for the other; but it is more logical to say that neither can exist without the other. The knower therefore, must either have relation to the known in all its parts or be a constituent half of the known by reflective or polarized opposition. This being understood, the problem of knowledge is shifted to the question of part and whole. Why is knowledge ever limited, if the subject bears a constant and indefeasible relation to all of the object? How can knowledge expand or contract; or, to put it another way, what is the law under which sensations and experiences come into and depart from consciousness? This brings us to the question of the nature of interest and attention. They are matters we cannot treat here. For psychology, knowledge either partial or complete consists in a polarized relation between subject and object. The amount of territory included in consciousness must in some way depend upon the intensity of the polarization and fluctuate with its rhythms.

4. Polarity and the Law of Opposites.

By polarity we mean the unity in opposites. The simplest expression of polarity is seen in the mathematical signs of plus and minus or in the physical phenomenon of the positive and negative poles of a magnet. The characteristics manifested are always diametrically opposed, but the tendency to exhibit opposite or contrasted properties is in the unit. What you can posit of one pole you can never posit of the other. Although polarity consists in possessing contrary tendencies, or powers in opposite or contrasted directions, it is the opposite aspects of a one thing.

This separation of things into opposite poles is not confined to physics. Although polarity pervades nature, it is equally characteristic of mental phenomena. Ideas and metaphysical conceptions are so constantly polarized that faint-hearted philosophers stagger at the problem of knowledge, fearing that all conceptions contradict or cancel each other. With fuller understanding the conviction arises that they, in fact, support or balance each other. How these concepts arise, with what distinctness they stand out, or in what way they show fluctuations in tension or energy is a question purely philosophical. It is sufficient to say that all discovered laws and principles are formulated in terms of these paradoxical concepts and that they seem to constitute the very framework of reality.

Subject and object are only one of many faithful pairs of opposites. Ideas in common use are as hopelessly antithetical as are metaphysical conceptions. Space is divided into its up and down, right and left and forward and backward. Time has its past and future balanced in the present. The idea of fast and slow also applies to time. Motion and rest, heat and cold, hard and soft, good and bad, and one and many are all polarized expressions.

Some of these concepts seem to blend into others, and some, like part and whole, motion and rest, light and dark, conscious and unconscious, stand out with such vividness and intensity that it would seem the very secret of existence had been compressed into the single term.

Notwithstanding the necessity of recognizing the system existing in these concepts, most philosophers have failed to observe their importance or to study them as a whole. They often encounter difficulty in detecting even the single pair of opposites involved in the simple object of search. Struggle after struggle takes place over opposite aspects of the same thing. Nor is that the only confusion, for each investigator may shift to an auxiliary pair of opposites or find himself at the reverse pole of his problem without himself being aware of how he made the change. For these reasons we wish to formulate the doctrine of the law of opposites so that the dual nature of all concepts may be anticipated and deliberately sought and understood. And by this very law of opposites the matter will not rest here. A surd or irreducible element will be implied in every polarized thing. This is probably the point of contact of the thing or conception with polarity of a different power or degree.

5. Mind and Matter as Polarized Aspects of the Same Thing.

We are now ready to state the hypothesis which will govern in formulating the principles contained in this book. The assumption or hypothesis which seems necessary in order to make psychology consistent and scientific is that mind and matter are opposite poles of the same thing. With this conception even tentatively accepted, so many difficult problems will be solved that we fearlessly advance into the most resistant and intricate territory. No question can be so obscure but that we shall be able to pick up either the mental or physical end of it. If it yields so far, we can, by the law of opposites, discover its antithetical companion. All that throws light on matter will illuminate mind. Every law discovered in the mental realm will have its reverse aspect and reflection in matter.

The application of the foregoing must, as with all hypotheses, be its justification. The real point at issue is whether nature has an internal aspect. By the hypothesis she has, and must exhibit her inmost secrets to all who have the courage and strength to question her. It is not logical nor consistent to assert completeness in a single pole. The material world with its myriads of specialized forms is bleak and barren without knowledge of their inner unity. The heart or mind wearied of the conflict of ideas and desires, by knowing the law of its being, may turn towards peace. Whether specialized in matter or generalized in thought, there will be one world, perceived and understood by countless minds. By the hypothesis, Minds are the Units of Force in which nature expresses herself as conscious.

CHAPTER I.

Consciousness.

1. Consciousness as a Whole having Parts.

The nature and characteristics of mind appear to us through consciousness. We study mind by observing its conscious processes, and by noting the laws governing its manifestations. Being the reverse side of matter, mind is as complex as matter, and is subject to every law operating in matter. It is the internal aspect of nature. Both matter and mind originate in a primal polarity of the substance of nature.

Let us consider some of the properties of matter and see the form they take at the pole of mind. Matter is always conceived as made up of particles or parts. Nature is a whole made up of parts. Science has not discovered the ultimate unit of matter. Atoms are not final units as long as they are conceived as having appreciable dimensions or geometrical shape. Even experimental science seems now to find that they break up into particles many times smaller in size than the atom was originally supposed to be. Atoms and ions, then, are just as arbitrary units as molecules, cells, organs, individuals or worlds.

But if matter is composed of parts, it is also a whole. Force is constant; matter is indestructible. Particles of matter always form a larger something which may be grasped in consciousness as a whole. Not only this, but all matter tends to take form and work itself out in an organized way. The tendency to relational adjustments is inherent in matter of all grades. In one form, the question is to find out what it is that unites all particles of matter in a living relation. What unity exists between the apparently discrete particles of matter so that each can bear a dynamic relation to the other? How can atoms be separated and have motion?

In answering the last question, we come to understand consciousness. The word conscious means to know with or against. A state of consciousness is impossible for a single unit of energy. Friction with another, or others, is essential to this condition. The conscious being is along with or against something and therefore limited and affected by it. Consciousness implies action and reaction, an interchange of force. There is a coalescence of subject with object, the me with the not-me, the see-er with the thing seen, the inner with the outer.

The relation between units of force, which makes possible this interdealing, is imperishable, but the force displayed in the contact defines the field of attention and divides consciousness into its parts. The extent of consciousness is always measured in terms of energy. Its content and mood vary with the forces brought into play. If there is no dealing with or bombardment of other units, there will be no action or reaction to produce life, and no friction to be measured as consciousness. The field of consciousness, then, is limited by the energy generated by the unit, and expands and contracts as this energy is given forth or conserved. The true unit cannot be added to or taken from. It expresses its characteristics and properties by polarization. The field of consciousness is the internal aspect of the unit's experiences. There is no polarity without dynamic tension or play of force between the poles. This tension or relation between mind and matter appears as consciousness. Through it we recognize the one thing polarized into parts.

To become conscious is an instantaneous process; if process at all. An individual lifts his eyelids in no matter what environment, whether hateful or likable, and becomes one with it, is glued to it, is the other half of it. It is recognition rather than cognition. He goes through no process of thought in regard to it, until after he has married it. He and his environment are one. He is conscious with the help of his environment; such reason as he brings to bear on the matter cuts no figure. The eyelids lift and the individual finds the other half of himself, his environment. Or with the physical eyes closed, the mental eyes may be opened upon an objective domain within the mind, either conjured by the imagination or recorded by memory. Whatever it is, it has been taken in from without sometime, somewhere. And at once the eye coalesces with it and becomes conscious; made so by the friction of the me and the not-me, of subject and object. However you look at the question, there must be at least two to make that state called consciousness. A unit unpolarized can never be conscious. If the center is everywhere and the circumference nowhere, each unit would seem to be the center of his own universe. But this is hard to conceive, although the countless differentiated and specialized forms make it necessary. As the many must be infinite, where can the Unit poise? Upon an alleged center? It were better to say, that the Unit is simply the conscious point, or point of consciousness, in its infinite environment. Whether this environment be conscious or not, it is not necessary to decide. The unit of energy, that is self-conscious, is fully aware that it could not be so without some environment. It is evident, then, that polarity is essential to consciousness, and that consciousness is not an act of reason, but instantaneous recognition.

Having explained how consciousness arises and is supported, let us examine its subdivisions and separation into parts. By the hypothesis, consciousness must have the same number of parts as matter. Every unit of matter has its mental pole resulting in an interposed moment or element of consciousness. If these cohere, there must be a world or cosmic consciousness embracing all matter. Evidently this is the case, but we now grasp it only by pushing our conceptions to their limit. Consciousness as we first pick it up for study has a definite and limited content. So the problem for psychology is to understand how consciousness can be less than the whole and more than the simplest sensation. How can dynamic tension or pressure result in fluctuations in the content of consciousness? Is there possible any separation of physical particles or isolation of consciousness? This question must be divided so that it can be answered in two ways.

Consciousness as studied by psychology is always the consciousness of an individual or true unit. It is the mind of one whose world expands or contracts with his desires. We speak of sub-, super-, and self-consciousness, or of under-, over-, and central-consciousness. This is really a play upon words. There is but one consciousness, and that is self-consciousness. We speak of the sum total of all consciousness, that is again fallacious. There can be no sum total of an infinity of self-consciousness. The limitless can never be summed. There is but one order of consciousness and that is self-consciousness. Its unity lies in the quality, its variety in the infinity of the units and the degrees of intensity of the sensations. The quality of consciousness then is one (self-consciousness) the quantity many, as innumerable as the units of force. Thus when we speak of super-consciousness and sub-consciousness we mean only some aspect of a larger self-consciousness than that with which we are accustomed to deal. That is, the unit-self within us expands to a larger recognition of environment than before. Instead of confining itself to a small room, it may coalesce with the visible universe, becoming less intense but more universal. As extreme meets extreme, and subject clashes with object, there is a subtle friction, (though friction is hardly the word) followed by neutralization in unity which is instantaneous recognition. Unity is never conscious, but the coming into unity is intense consciousness. Subject and object are forever merging and consciousness results. The symbol is that of the serpent with its tail in its mouth. The head recognizes the tail of the one body which unites the two.

Consciousness, measured by the impulses of force, shades off in intensity at rhythmic periods. Not only that, but it passes to the opposite pole of unconsciousness. This retreating from outer to inner environment is most commonly recognized in sleep. The ego goes farther and farther back into itself until the outer environment is lost. What new environment is reached, we need not say. The important point is that reversing of consciousness is not only possible but necessary. Nature forces it upon us, but that realm may be deliberately sought. For every vale without there is one within. Every prospect of mountain or sea can be matched within. The sun, the stars, constellation upon constellation, system upon system, the universe itself, each is interior as well as exterior. and may be reached by consciousness from either direction.

Having considered the matter from the standpoint of our hypothesis, we come to the conclusion that consciousness is a whole having parts. It is a whole, because the Unit of Force never loses its unitary character. It has parts, because the contact of the Unit with other Units produces an infinite variety of sensations which result in changes in the field of consciousness.

By close analysis, we find consciousness subtly complex. An individual seems to be simultaneously conscious of many things. Bodily sensations, mental efforts and emotional reactions unite in the stream of consciousness and color all its waters. Realizing the gamut of being from the crudest forms of matter to the subtlest processes of mind, consciousness passes through all shadings and gradations, meets all forms of the manifested universe and coalesces with its moods, altogether equal to the other half of itself. The fact of consciousness proves the indestructibility of the Units. There is no consciousness without the many; a conscious **One** is impossible. The Law of Consciousness necessitates eternally conscious Units. The whole of consciousness unites all the parts.

2. Sensation as Contact between Units of Force.

It seems well established that the five senses of seeing, hearing, tasting, smelling and feeling are but differentiated forms of the tactile sense, which is but a means to facilitate contact and consciousness. The nexus that unites subject and object is primarily touch. Touch, when analyzed, is seen to be a means of discerning resistance and motion. Experimenters recognize this, and call attention to the direct consciousness of muscular effort, resistance and motion, even suggesting that these forms of sensations are received by a special sense. The number of special senses discovered makes little difference. All sensations unite in consciousness and are specializations of consciousness. For this reason we have treated of consciousness first. The simplest element in consciousness is sensation.

Sensation, as we know it, arises only by means of organs of sense. Sense organs are composed of matter. They are evolved by the process of evolution, and, from the matter side, are controlled by physical laws. They correspond to portions of the physical environment and make possible the constant adjustment of the living organisms thereto. Bearing this in mind, we define sensation as conscious contact between Units of Force. By Units of Force we mean units which have the double aspect of matter and mind. From the viewpoint of matter, there are only aggregates of matter or particles of matter. From the viewpoint of mind, there are only units of sensation or centers of consciousness. By Units of Force, however, we mean polarized units. At one pole they are conscious and have sensations. At the other pole they have form and manifest the characteristics of matter. The word Unit implies substance and the word Force implies contact and interdealing. Out of the contact of the Units of Force arises sensation. Only through their interdealing is conscious life possible.

3. The Rhythms of Expansion and Contraction of Consciousness.

Starting with any given state of consciousness, it is manifest that the content does not remain the same. Activity is followed by repose. Attention and alert observation are overcome by drowsiness and want of interest. This applies not only to the larger rhythms of waking and sleeping, youth and old age, but to every single sensation and object in consciousness. All objects in consciousness wax and wane.

Seeing this expansion and contraction of the field of consciousness, we ask what is the cause. Let us take the simplest illustrations, for consciousness as exhibited in man is very complex. Considering sight, we see that the apparent size of all objects depends upon their distance from the observer in space and their illumination. Without change in the space relations with reference to the object seen, the visual power of the observer at least subjectively may be momentarily increased or diminished. Also, up to a certain point, familiarity with an object brings a quicker detection of it and a clearer discernment in consciousness. The diminishing value in consciousness caused by distance applies also to objects observed with reference to light and heat given off, irrespective of size. Distance also tends to decrease the volume of sound.

The above mentioned variations in consciousness are observed by simple experiments. From them we conclude that space and time elements constantly modify conscious states. Consciousness is measured on a sliding scale. Fluctuations may come from the outer environment or from the inner organ. The cause of the fluctuations is change in space relations and in rapidity of vibrations. The matter presented being complex, consciousness varies constantly. Objects are sensed by pulsations of attention. Rhythms of waking and sleeping affect all life. The periodic laws governing the motions of matter have their correlative expression in moods and states of consciousness.

4. The Seat of Consciousness in the Physical Body.

Consciousness, as we define the term, includes all mental processes, so that if we discover its seat in the body, we also have the location of sensations of the emotions and of thought. By our hypothesis, however, we are excluded from assigning consciousness to an exclusive locality. It arises from contact and friction between Units of Force, and therefore has no locality, but that of the Units. This is true to the facts as far as observed. The vibrations received by sense-organs are but specialized forms of the impulses and waves of motion undulating in spirals through all nature. Sensation arises for the Unit only when it resists or modifies them. Sensations, emotions and thoughts correspond to the motions of the matter composing the Unit's vehicle of expression. The motion is the physical pole, the sensation the mental pole of the same thing.

This being the case, the point in any wave of motion at which sensation arises for the individual depends upon the organization of his physical vehicle and the intensity and focus of his attention. Many Units of Force participate in the motions of the same physical body, yet with varying degrees of consciousness. The physical body is an aggregate presided over and dominated by resident forces. Changes in physical particles and cellular structure make no difference, because the Unit of Force is not the particular physical body of any moment, but the co-ordinating energy under the impulses of which the physical particles assume their positions. The physical body being the temporary expression of the Unit, the scope and character of its consciousness depend upon the energy of the Unit and the state of fruition of the causes set in operation by it. Its immediate consciousness is measured by the intensity of its desires and the direction towards which it turns its attention. A shifting focus of attention and interest may extend its consciousness above or below the normal, that is to say, to any and all vibrations in which the Unit participates.

States of consciousness and the vehicle of expression change together. Each may grow greater or less, become complex or simple. Differentiation within the physical body brings variety in consciousness but cannot furnish it a new nor exclusive seat. The extent of consciousness depends upon the energy given forth by the Unit, the quality upon the portions of its environment appropriated. By ceasing to set in motion causes of its own, any Unit of Force may fall in with the activities and consciousness of other Units and penetrate to the consciousness of subtler processes and greater harmonies than it is capable of alone.

In this paragraph we have spoken of physical bodies and vehicles. Strictly speaking there are no bodies or vehicles except physical. Under our hypothesis we can seek no other. Force must operate in matter, however subtle or fine. Matter and material forms are always manifestations of mind. It follows, therefore, that there can be no consciousness without a physical vehicle. All bodies and all extended and visible forms are manifestations of some grade of consciousness. There is no motion in matter without its expression at the pole of mind. There is no mind or consciousness but that which arises out of material contact and friction. Neither is without the other. The permanence of one preserves all mutations of the other.

In this paragraph we have not discussed in detail the relation the unit bears to organs of sense. All matter in motion having a conscious aspect, we say organs of sense are only convenient methods of responding to vibrations. A unit of force does not consciously come in direct contact with all the activities of other units, but receives the motions through others in modified forms. If the unit shows an aptitude or inclination in any direction. it will respond to the vibrations that come to it from that source and an appropriate sense organ will be evolved, of which organ many other units will form a part. The sensation reaches the dominant unit through these assistants. The sensation arises by reason of the modification of the matter of which they are composed, but the sense organ is what it is on account of the force displayed and the tension imposed by the dominant unit. This being the case, any impact affecting the sense organ invades the field of force of the unit and is thus felt. If it is a sensation of importance, numerous actions, reactions and special adjustments quickly follow. They in turn may give rise to new sensations. The consciousness of the unit arises from the motion of the matter within its field of force and which is dominated by its poles.

5. Abnormal Aspects of Consciousness.

We have seen how consciousness is dependent upon the motion of matter, and how matter has motion by reason of its unity in mind. The invisible side of matter is mind. The visible side of mind is matter. Neither mind nor matter exists alone. They are opposite poles of the same thing. From this it follows that all motion in matter has appropriate expression in consciousness. All vibrating particles are the external manifestation of some grade of consciousness. The forces of nature are generated by Units of Force.

This being the case, by our hypothesis, there should be levels and octaves of consciousness. This appears true to the facts. All unusual and abnormal forms of consciousness have to do with higher or lower manifestations of consciousness and with phenomena from which the average person is shut out by a kind of insulation. The rate of vibration may be too high or too low for detection, or the insulation may be too great.

There are two classes of persons on whom these unusual vibrations impinge so as to awaken a focused consciousness. First, those who are momentarily out of adjustment with their dominant environment. Second, those who from any cause have developed a special sensitiveness. It makes no difference to which class the observer belongs. The forms seen and the sensations received are caused by vibrations in matter of some grade, and at some rate. The mathematics of consciousness extends to all its planes.

There is another phase of this matter not usually borne in mind. The rhythms of nature produce countless tones and overtones which form a part of our consciousness. These notes are ordinarilly not heard and the effect of most vibrations pass unperceived, but their influence is none the less constant. If taken away, their loss would be at once recognized. The mood and complexion of our whole state of consciousness would be changed.

From the foregoing we conclude that abnormality is only relative. Scattered and unbalanced forms may be galvanized into temporary vehicles of consciousness, but are only temporary manifestations of the Unit of Force. The injection of phenomena into the experience of one person which others cannot ordinarily verify needs no special explanation. Whether from within or without, it is caused by matter in motion. In either case it can be perceived by others sufficiently sensitive or who sufficiently identify themselves with the person having the experience. It will produce consciousness in any Unit that resists it sufficiently to establish a definite check or tension. Having shown in what abnormality consists, the question still remains as to what occasions the sensitiveness or unbalance which brings about the unusual experience or the unaccustomed action.

In the normal condition, the Ego meets and coalesces with the non-ego placidly, without special heat or emotion. There is a calm participation in the events in a harmonious environment. If, for any reason, the feeling becomes more intense with reference to another person or thing, the intensity seldom rises beyond safe and exhilarating enthusiasm. Such a person may be a poet, artist musician or orator. Although accustomed to climaxing his emotions, he descends gracefully to the dead level of humanity in a proper and well-balanced manner. A normal man does even unusual things in a normal way. His acts co-ordinate. Their causes and effects are a perfect fit and easily discerned. He would be a genius without eccentricities. His judgment as to when concentration upon any subject should stop would be superb.

There is, however, another class of persons who are thrown upon the outer edge of events and things. When organs begin to disintegrate and institutions change, there are those who first feel the process and react against it. Once broken from moorings, the effect upon each individual varies greatly. One will adapt himself to a changing environment without offense to those of either the old or the new order of things. In him sensitiveness and action combine with poise. Another, not having himself under control, will run into excess of every kind. He overuses and abuses his power. He concentrates all his energy on what he desires without regard to the results that follow, without considering the effect upon others. Once launched on a given course, it is only a question of time until he reaches an unusual environment and begins unusual experiences. If his excesses consist in the use of drugs, stimulants or narcotics, he will suppress certain functions of body and mind and stimulate others. If he gives way to passional or emotional excesses, appropriate results will follow. If he becomes fascinated with mental problems, and subjects himself to the forces that play upon sensitive brains and nerves, he may be sucked into unknown depths of the maelstroms of nature's subtle currents. Whichever way he turns he can penetrate to the abnormal. Having arrived at unusual experiences, he is ill-fitted to describe them. He has no sense of proportion, no fixed standard of value. The thing gazed at becomes so large in his entranced mind that all outside of it sinks into non-entity. The glasses he wears distort and discolor all he views. The normal individual scoffs at his incoherent tales.

In spite of this, the abnormal is the most valuable comment on the normal. Pathological processes first attract attention. In investigating them, we are led to investigate ordinary phenomena and to discern their true nature. There are recurrent states in all individuals that partake of the intensity and isolation of the abnormal. The lover for a time disregards the rights of others, neglects his person, forgets to eat, and is unable to sleep. He sees nothing but the loved eyes and hears nothing but the loved voice. Should this state of infatuation continue, it would amount to a selfishness intolerable to the rest of mankind. The mother during the infancy of her child is abnormally concentrated upon it. It is a wise provision of nature for the child's protection, but should this state of mind continue in her until the child has reached full growth, the maternal instinct would have eclipsed and left to atrophy her other powers. As the child grows more able to help itself, however, the mother reverts to her original condition and her normal self is saved from extinction.

Abnormal concentration as a rule leads to vacuity and brings evil results, but sometimes it digs out a jewel of superlative value or discovers a principle that reforms a race. It defies earth, ancestors, conventionality and prudence. The abnormally concentrated mind, acting intellectually or emotionally, may shake the world; it may also lead to madness and individual ruin.

Moods are certain aspects of concentration in consciousness. They may have their way until the will is swallowed by them and an unfocused vagueness and dissipation of power result. In hypnotism concentration is followed by a reaction that takes the subject to the pole of sleep or trance. There is a loss of balance of polarity in consciousness in all forms of mental derangement.

Having referred to some phases of mental unbalance and abnormal concentration of consciousness, let us consider a normal growth in sensitiveness to vibrations ordinarily ignored. Consciousness being dominated by rhythmic impulses, the sensitiveness would appear at the crest of certain waves and disappear with the receding tide. As an appropriate organ is formed to sense the alien vibrations, the consciousness of them would become possible. As consciousness is raised to and maintained focused at the requisite level they would be constantly in mind. We conclude, therefore, that all differences between individuals in their power to receive impressions depend upon differences in the development and range of sensitiveness of their sense organs and upon the available energy and intensity of their concentration. Whether arising internally or externally, the phenomena will be the result of vibrations and will be sensed by reason of the modifications they cause in some organ dominated by the Unit and within its field of force. What this magic consciousness is no man can tell save he who realizes it; but the law by which it works may be discovered. Whether the manifestations be normal or abnormal, the principle of polarity of our hypothesis, in its countless forms, will hold true.

CHAPTER II.

Desire.

1. Energy is Directed by Desire.

Having seen how consciousness is dependent upon contact and interdealing between Units of Force, we shall now treat of the energy that makes motion possible and of desire which gives direction to energy.

Inasmuch as minds are Units of Force which generate energy according to their ability, it is important to consider how the energy is directed. Like all forces, energy is invisible and from the matter pole is seen only in its results. It may be accumulated or discharged, conserved or given forth. Whether kinetic or latent, it is generated by some Unit and limited by the capacity of the generator. Knowing the power of any given Unit to generate energy, the importance of its relation to given processes can be determined and its possible effect on specific phenomena calculated. Speaking in terms of mathematics, the energy which the Unit can manifest is fixed by the position assumed by it in the vibratory matrix which gives birth to the phenomena manifested. In other words, all evolution is under the impulse of dominant rhythms participated in by graduated forces.

Before proceding further in the elucidation of our hypothesis we wish to refer to the insufficiency of language to express fully our idea. Words are but symbols, and sometimes very inadequate to envelope a thought. Nevertheless, we shall try to make our position as clear as the vocabulary will allow. Strictly speaking, we cannot refer to force in unity or the unity of force without tautology, force being its own creation and beyond comprehension. When we strive to express our idea of it as a unit's power or capacity to generate energy we are in reality saying, "Force generates force;" in fact we are in the realm of the unspeakable as well as the unthinkable. Though we strictly maintain the constancy of force and believe that from the point of relativity of balance there is no adding to or taking from it possible, that is, that a unit is absolutely, mathematically true to itself in its capacity for generating energy through its relation to environment, yet in spite of this we shall continually through this work speak of the dissipation, accumulation, etc., of energy as though it could be increased or diminished. Force is constant, but the forms in which it may appear as energy are innumerable.

In common parlance we must use these terms, for, in common parlance, we speak specially and not from a sweeping generalization or completed unity. For all intents and purposes from the point of human consciousness energy does accelerate, diminish and transfer itself. It is quite unessential that we go into a discussion here of what in the final analysis these terms really mean. We refer to our use of them only to show we are not contradicting ourselves when we say on the same page that force is constant and its manifestation as energy inconstant.

If there were not things there would be nothing, not even force, for what is energy but a resultant from a clash of desires in **things?** Without things there would be no motion, for what is motion but a result of energy or force which again results from individual desires? Without **things** there would be no desire, for what is desire but a unit will focused upon another of its kind? But when we generalize upon these same indispensable **things** that make the terms energy, motion, will, etc., in a sense understandable, we find that from the point of relationship they are mathematically limited as to power, motion and gratification of this same desire; and not that only, for besides being stable and fixed in capacity, and as though the number of each were stamped upon it, they through the vibrations which they excite in each other seem to lose and transfer their energy. To be sure, this, from the fact of their relationship, is only seeming; yet, for the purpose of conscious life it is a loss or gain, and in argument we must envelope the subject with the terms of instability. Having thus tried to make clear our two positions, sometimes arguing from the peak of generalization, and again from the plain of specialization, one can readily throughout this psychology compare the two senses in which these terms are used and preserve the balance of meaning to which the two aspects of the matter correspond.

What has just been said applies only to the fixed characteristic or power of the Unit to generate a constant but limited amount of energy. The direction in which this energy may be sent, or whether it shall be given forth or conserved, is not the same thing as the power to generate it. The power to generate a constant amount of energy being characteristic of the Unit, there must be some principle or law governing the direction given to the energy and the purposes it may be made to serve. The law to which we refer is that energy is the servant of will or desire and may be directed towards the accomplishment of any purpose. Purposes, however, are of necessity confined to a field created by the Units. Desire is meaningless except as it goes out to others.

2. Attraction and Repulsion between Units of Force.

From the pole of mind, all motion originates in attraction and repulsion between Units of Force. Observed from the standpoint of matter, the motion is towards or from a given point, but the mental element consists in the desire or aversion that accompanies the action. Assuming that all phenomena are products of the interdealing of Units, the question arises as to why there should be interdealing and why one contact should be pleasant and another painful. There must be some law which necessitates the interdealing. There must be some principle which determines the quality of the resulting emotion.

Inasmuch as matter and mind are opposite poles of the same thing, there is no possibility for interdealing or room for experience except between Units of Force. This being without exception, there is no choice in the matter except as to the time and manner of acting or reacting and the amount of energy displayed.

In its simplest terms, desire is a creative effort directed towards having certain experiences or prolonging other experiences. Its opposite pole is aversion, and aversion seeks to avoid or suppress experiences. The positive or creative pole is desire, the negative or regulative pole of the rhythm is satiety or aversion. The negative pole, therefore, cannot be reached except by way of the positive. All phenomena from the matter side being measured by vibrations, we conclude that the pleasurable or painful quality of an experience is dependent upon the harmony or irregularity of its rhythms, and the intensity upon the rapidity of the motion. Harmonic forms and waves of motion tend to reproduce themselves indefinitely, while discord tends ever towards pain, silence and death. It is evident, therefore, that Units of Force are attracted by harmonic vibrations and are repelled by those which disturb the pleasing forms within their fields of force. Under the law which lays upon them the necessity for specialization they seek and find countless experiences. Out of the mathematics of their environments arise appropriate pleasure and pain.

Desire, then, is a universal attribute of subject in its relation to object. It goes out from subjectivity to objectivity, for the ego-subject can never wish anything of itself. There can be no consciousness without desire or will. Shut out all interested contact or dealing with the inner or outer environment, and to all experiences of sense and intellect the unit becomes dead. In multiplicity of experiences in the objective world, operating through desire, is life found. Desire and desire only makes conscious life possible.

Desire operates immediately and directs energy in a straight line. It would bear all before it in a single impulse of energy. It consents to no deviation until the crest of the wave is reached. It is checked only by counter desires or by pushing the experience to satiety. The impulses of desire meeting desire produce spirals of motion. Only in the climaxes of rhythm is fruition reached.

3. The Poles of Desire.

The first outrush of energy under the domination of desire is always pleasurable. Desire or will is free and sovereign. It is the initiator of conscious life, the universal priest that marries subject to object. By the union is brought forth light and all splendor of consciousness.

We must understand, however, that desire is not the force usually exerted to bring about its gratification. Force is neutral and measured by quantity. All energy may be transformed. Desire enables man to realize his environment, but the perfect attainment of a particular desire is in a large measure impossible. Of necessity man finds his limitation in the other pole of himself known as environment. Objective forms can be appropriated and realized only by the expenditure of the same amount of force as dominates them. There is no limit to what one may desire. The attainment of desire, however, is dependent upon the amount of energy available for the purpose. Within the citadel of subjectivity will is sovereign. In the realm of objectivity, countless hands reach for the guiding scepter. It is a struggle of forces in which the greater energy will prevail.

In passing from subjectivity to objectivity the monarch will is inevitably dethroned. In the world of objective things gratification is never complete. Desire knows nothing of complete fulfillment. A desire fulfilled is a desire annihilated. That desire is suicidal that seeks complete gratification. The true function of desire is to make the poles of being conscious of each other. Through subject realizing object, life itself becomes possible. Out of it finally comes orderly sequence, comprehension and understanding. If desire is responsible for life, it must also account for death. Unpolarized desire would be a force acting in a straight line. It would be without limit and would show no variety in consciousness. For all desires, however, there is a turning point where satiety and aversion is reached. This is inevitable under the law of polarity. The fulcrum or base from which the desire operates accumulates and carries as a balanced and polarized product all effects of which desire has been the cause. Satisfied desires pass out of consciousness until the effects return as causes and the old experience is revived in consciousness in its polarized aspect. Passing through infinity it has changed its sign. It is seen, therefore, that the positive pole of desire is consciousness and pleasure, and the negative pole aversion and pain. Unconsciousness is timeless. We know only that it shuts out from us experiences of which others are conscious. Of them we also may be conscious at another time, or on another and differently polarized plane.

What causes desire first to emerge it is useless to say. Desire is the father of all causes, a fixed element in the consciousness of the units. It both creates and is created by their contact and friction. Its operation affects all motion and determines the quality of action and reaction. It is responsible for adjustment between organism and environment, and is the inner force directing all evolution and change. It is polarity itself, the cause of all separation and the giver forth of that which returns after many days.

When specialized, desire is an act of appropriation. When generalized, it is from the matter pole the gravitation that holds all physical particles in its embrace and from the mental pole the love and longing for unity that tends to harmonize all experiences. In one sense through desire we control objectivity, that is, we take it into consciousness and it becomes ours in possible and orderly adjustment. We sit centrally in a wheel of the universe and with kingly absorption dominate our world. In the almightiness of generalization, we are crowned and sceptered. But when the God descends into the maze of specialization, seeking to wed the mortal, he is nude, unsceptered and dethroned. To an extent his desire may be realized and annihilated, but everywhere he comes hard against limitations. Time, space, variety and complexity are his enemies. Rhythm entangles him. The God within is degraded, and passion, fear, hatred, lust, greed and revenge are the crops in this jungle that he harvests.

Yet far back in the essence of his being is primal desire or will, free, sovereign and unquenchable through its very nature of being. Desire finds its limitation only exteriorly in its attempted satisfaction and, therefore, in annihilation and death. The conclusion, then, is that desire attained is desire killed. Desire alive is unsatisfied and free, making comprehension of objectivity possible. It is a nexus between the poles of being, between free subjectivity and conditioned objectivity, and forced to remain alive because by the very nature of objectivity it is impossible that it should be completely gratified. Desire is primitive, initiatory, universal, the key to consciousness, and, therefore, life. To strive to kill, subdue or chastise the will, making it subservient to some other will, is in the last analysis a prayer for extinction. The surrender of individuality in morbid attempts of this kind ends in unconsciousness, trance, hypnotic sleep or death.

If man knows his limitations as well as his sovereignty he may wisely seek experience in objectivity. The game of life has its excitement and charm. The realm of specialized being burning with passion, intense with thought, shifting its panorama of seeming illusions, pyrotechnic in its play of light and shade, echoing with laughter and groans, a locality of pitfalls, mountain tops, oceans and skies, is the place where the Immortal finds his correllate, the mortal, where the God kisses the feet of necessity and learns the meaning of individuality, differentiation, relativity, time, space, variety and, therefore, of life.

4. The Effect of Will or Desire in Matter.

If will or desire gives direction to energy, then it affects matter directly. Being able to affect matter, it cannot operate without affecting it. There is no place where it can operate except in matter of some grade. This being the case, we must ask whether there can be any motion in matter which does not arise from the operation of will or desire. Reasoning from the known to the unknown, we conclude there is not. All motion of which we know results from attraction or repulsion, and these, on the mental side, are the expression of will or desire. Being a sufficient cause, we find no room for another. The chemical processes going on in low grades of matter are similar to the changes in the matter composing the highly evolved organs of man. We know his consciousness depends upon the motion of the particles. The same desire that directs and modifies them finds expression also in the less responsive matter of lower grade. We define matter, then, as the external manifestation of a specialized activity of will. Will is a first cause, shaping and finding expression in matter. Chemical elements are defined by the periodic functions of their atomic weights. Their characteristics are determined mathematically. Their existence is conditioned by vibrations in which any unit may participate. Their permanence is as a beam of light which shines into a room whenever the screen which neutralizes the constituent vibrations is withdrawn.

The variety and abundance of forms we see in nature are a result of freedom from interior limitations on the part of desire. Complete objective expression may be thwarted, but the impulse has been given and an appropriate form results. A cause has gone forth. Motion necessarily results until action and reaction are equal. Desire, therefore, works in every field. It is neither strong nor weak, but may use a great amount of energy or give impulse barely sufficient to arouse consciousness. For these reasons it is evident that there are all gradations of desire from vague and half-conscious longings, in which many participate, to the most specialized passions which can stir to action or arouse emotion.

5. Abnormal Aspects of Desire.

Desire may become abnormal and bring about a want of adjustment with environment in two ways: First, one may put such intensity into his thoughts or actions along a particular line as almost immediately to reach a position out of harmony with others. Second, he may over a long period of time direct a small amount of energy towards the gratification of some desire until the accumulated product will break forth and overwhelm him or morbidly dominate his thoughts and actions. In either case he will act in an unusual manner, and appear abnormal.

In spite of the great differences manifested, overmastering passions and morbid appetites have but one source. They are specialized forms of desire, their intensity depending upon the strength of the unit or the length of time he has directed energy towards the accomplishment of his purpose. In the case of accumulated emotions, it is evident that there is some suspension of the sequence of cause and effect, some interval before the reaction follows the original impulse. This is made possible by the participation of other units in the original emotions. Vibrations produced in any manner tend to awake corresponding vibrations in all beings at the same state of organization and tension. Having responded and acted in concert, they are under the influence of all recurring rhythms, each intensifying and enhancing the activity of the other until the climax of the experience is reached and the ebb flow of the tide sets in.

We conclude, therefore, that appetites are built up by the seeking of emotions not in themselves abnormal and that the most terrible of passions are manifestations of energy which may be controlled and directed in other channels of desire.

CHAPTER III.

Action and Reaction.

1. The Double Aspect of Physical and Mental Laws.

Inasmuch as mind and matter by our hypothesis are opposite poles of the same thing, we are at liberty to take up any important principle or concept and examine it from either aspect. All laws that have been established by physical science will have their expression at the mental pole. All principles regulating the operations of mind will be found to have a reverse aspect in the physical world. No definition of a law or principle can therefore be complete until the characteristics at each pole have been observed and the double aspect of its operation understood.

This being the case, all organisms and forms resulting from natural processes will have both an internal and an external aspect. The lowest grades of material substances have structural parts and characteristics determined by resident forces as truly as higher forms. We encounter polarity and the rhythms of action and reaction wherever we turn. It is this double nature of things that makes them what they are. Through polarity they expand into being, and the actions and reactions which constitute their life are nothing other than polarity expressed as motion and rhythm.

Considering polarity and rhythm as laws of universal application, we can understand why language must have a double aspect. It is the mediator between the physical and the mental. Facing both ways, it partakes of the characteristics of each. It is a means by which the vibrations in us which stand for the consciousness of some special thing are awakened in others who have had or are capable of having the same experiences. It is a specialized form of contact and intercourse between Units of Force. By means of it energy is given forth and received. It is thought and vibrations in matter at the same time. No vibrations in matter can be awakened except by Force. The experience of each individual tends to reproduce itself in all others. All vibrations in matter, whether of coarse or fine grade, go out until they reach the limit prescribed by the form of the conducting medium and in time inevitably return to their source.

This going forth and returning of the wave of vibration is the action and reaction which appears in all natural processes. Varied in form, often obscure in operation, it still is one of the greatest laws and is manifested both at the pole of matter and at the pole of mind.

2. Mathematical and Geometrical Symbols and Illustrations.

We stated in the preceding paragraph that vibrations in matter go out until they reach the limit prescribed by the form of the conducting medium and then return to their source. If this be true, it must also be true that there is no form of tension of material substances capable of producing vibrations which will not ultimately return the impulses to their source. We can make the matter clearer by illustrations.

The simplest vibrations we can observe are the oscillations of a pendulum. In a pendulum, we have the three elements of the fixed point of suspension, the cord which holds the weight up with the gravity which pulls the weight down, and the impulse from without which sets the pendulum in motion. Give the pendulum an impulse at right angles to its line of suspension and it will swing back and forth, its point tracing the segment of an arc of a circle. Were there no atmospheric or other friction, the pendulum would continue its motion without ceasing. At each oscillation it would return to and through the original point where the weight hung at rest, being also the point at which the impulse of energy was received. By every vibration, then, the whole amount of energy is returned to the point of origin. It requires the same energy to check the pendulum and take up its motion at this central point. That amount of force applied at any other point will produce a different result. If force is interposed at the extremity of the arc of vibration it can never neutralize the motion except under conditions of constant tension. The pendulum may be held at the limit of its swing by application of the same amount of energy that produced the motion, but when this force is withdrawn the pendulum carries back through the point of origin the energy undiminished. Apply force at any intermediate point of the arc, and you can increase or diminish the amplitude of the oscillations, but rest cannot be produced and the energy neutralized or withdrawn. Only at the point of origin may the energy be neutralized. At no other place can rest be permanent. Something will remain to be done. All causes are suspended in their effects until they return to their source.

What has been said of the oscillations of a pendulum would apply equally to the vibrations of a musical chord, or of an elastic plate. Another form in which the waves of action and reaction may be studied would be a sphere of liquid surface, as if the earth were evenly covered with water. In such a case, let an impulse be given at one pole to produce a wave. The wave would flow out towards the opposite pole, pass the equator at a uniform elevation, culminate at the negative pole, and there would be reversed and thrown back to the point of origin, only to have the oscillation repeated until the friction of the material and the interference of the secondary waves absorbed the original energy. Even when absorbed the energy would be latent and bear a causal relation to the original impulse.

We see, therefore, how it is that mathematical and geometrical symbols are the only illustrations we have of our profoundest principles and laws. In them polarity and causality are exemplified continually. Constant and invariable, they form the frame work of reality. On this skeleton is hung the flesh that makes living man. Only by understanding them can one fathom matter and mind.

3. Action and Reaction as a Psychological Law.

If mind and matter are opposite poles of the same thing, then we can observe the law of action and reaction at work in mental processes as well as in the physical world, although it will appear in reverse aspect. That which appears as **cause** at the physical pole will be **effect** at the mental, and that which is **effect** in the physical world will appear as will or **cause** in its internal aspect. If one aspect is positive the other is negative. If one pole appears as motion at the other pole will be rest. All motion is determined by positive and negative elements of force. The tendency is either centrifugal or centripetal. Action and reaction are always equal.

From the foregoing it follows that rhythm, psychologically speaking, may be reckoned mathematically. A high tide implies a low, and a medium activity implies a medium inactivity, or reaction. This law was so well understood by contemplative races, that before the time of Confucius the ancient Chinese "Book of Changes" was written to exemplify it, and that philosopher understood its importance and enlarged upon the theme. By the law of rhythm, the future was forecast. Reactions in the seasons, in diseases, and in all psychological experiences were estimated by the intensity of the action.

Although founded upon the simplest and most easily demonstrated of laws, this famous book became, to the ignorant, an occult scroll, teeming with unreasoned prophecy and forcing the future to lift its veil. At first incredulous and without capacity to understand, by the same law of rhythm they passed to the opposite pole of superstition and credulity.

It is startling to observe in every day life how little men take stock of their reactions. They gloat upon deeds, and strenuous activities, forgetting the ebb tide while on the waves of the high. They plan for great things; ignoring practically the fact that the negative shadow accompanies the positive light, and not knowing that they will fall asleep beneath the eaves of their unfinished structure, some to be killed by its fall upon their heads. Man should change all this and coolly calculate profit and loss, or the action and reaction accompanying every enterprise in which he engages. His output of energy means its corresponding return and he should estimate all things on this basis. Rhythm affects environment outside of himself as well as himself. The complexity of life is produced by the interference of different rythms at the various stages of high and low tide. These tremendously complicated interactions must be calculated by the seeker after poise. Only those who understand the law can balance action with reaction and determine the periodic return of a given wave.

Without a due consideration of rhythm, psychology is a body without its head. That which makes calculation possible is left out. It can never determine the "psychological moment," and therefore will not grasp it. Rhythm is the key to a balanced psychology, although most difficult of application. At the acute point of specialized action, the slightest deviation misses the mark. From the base of a broad generalization, the results are apparent and sure.

4. Accumulated Causes and Suspended Results.

Action and reaction always being equal, it follows that, knowing a cause and the conditions under which it acts, we can compute the result; perceiving a result, we can find out the cause. There are no phenomena without causes. There are no causes that do not produce effects.

The relation between cause and effect, as we understand it, is not the same as the rhythms of action and reaction. Action and reaction, psychologically defined, are the changes within the Unit of Force by reason of some particular activity. Cause and effect are terms better applied to designate co-ordinated changes in two or more Units arising out of the same contact and interdealing. Causality, in this sense, always bears an exterior aspect, action and reaction an interior. Rhythm, therefore, applies only to action and reaction. Cause and effect, being strictly co-ordinated, are timeless.

This being the case, the accumulated causes and suspended results of which we speak are within the Unit. There is no storing up of forces elsewhere. There can be no suspension of results in another place. The forces which surround us with invisible tendencies arise within. Those things which affect us, or can affect us, are a part of us. Our actions in the complicated environment which surrounds us create a larger self in which all transactions form and outline themselves until the returning wave brings back the energy to the Unit of Force and the rhythm is completed and closed.

The distinctions here referred to are not inconsistent with the common sense view of the external world. Although the action and reaction is within the Unit, the same activity may appear as cause and effect between other Units. This is the exterior view which ignores the suspended interior reaction. Being thus limited, it fails to account for half the problems of life. When action and reaction are fully understood, each one will know that all energy given forth returns to the giver, whenever a passive state makes it possible, rendering exact account of all it has wrought.

5. Abnormal Aspects of Action and Reaction.

The law of action and reaction being of universal application, it follows that the ordinary actions of men, produced by only moderately energetic efforts, are accompanied by only moderate reactions and results. The effect in the external world is not marked. The interior reaction is not startling. There are two ways, however, by which extraordinary and abnormal results may be brought about. One is by the process of insulation of the energy tending in a given direction, until it accumulates pressure to break all barriers and escape as a full grown cause. The other method is that in which the Unit of Force devotes all its energy to the production of an immediate result, regardless of propriety or consequences. At the time of observing the action, it may be hard to determine which process was involved. The strength and impulsiveness of the action may appear abnormal although no law has been violated or contravened.

The ability to accumulate energy, here referred to, is of highest importance. By means of it almost any object comes within reach of one who desires it sufficiently. If not possessed of strength to gain his purpose at once, it is only necessary that he forego the expenditure of energy in the pursuit of other objects until enough is accumulated to gain this paramount desire. If confined, the pressure will rise until it becomes irresistible. When an object is not desired with an intensity that ignores all else, little difference does it make what magnitude of events may be necessary to bring to others their joys and sorrows.

In all action and reaction is involved a time feature which is closely connected with the insulation that makes accumulation of energy possible. Insulation, under the control of the Unit, is one factor. The time element, resulting from the sequence of events occasioned by the nature of the rhythm, is the other. The quantity of energy and the mass involved in the rhythm must always be considered. Out of those elements arises on the mental side what corresponds to voltage or pressure on the physical. Insulation is also expressed in terms of polarity, being the opposite of contact and interdealing. Contact and interdealing are meaningless except as implying an isolation alternately enforced and suspended. Here the principles of motion and rest commingle. Viewed statically, the idea is that of the Many and the One.

CHAPTER IV.

Emotion.

1. Emotion accompanies Energy.

We have seen in the preceding chapters how consciousness depends upon the motion of matter and how motion in matter is caused by desire or will. Desire, or its equivalent in the various orders of nature, is a constantly working cause producing motion in matter and the appropriate attendant consciousness. This motion and interdealing being between Units of Force the law of action and reaction intervenes and becomes a fixed form and characteristic of the motion, and therefore a law applying to both its mental and physical aspects. We have seen further that energy is directed by desire, being its constant servant. Bearing this in mind, we will now treat of emotion and the feelings that accompany energy as given forth and directed by desire.

Like all forces, the energy inherent in the unit follows the laws of conservation of energy and transformation of energy. The forces of the units are the forces of nature and therefore consistent with natural laws. All that we can learn of the pressure and tension of gases, of hydraulic power, of the laws governing electrical and chemical energy will be knowledge of the energy of the Units and a commentary on its mode of operation. All their manifestations will have a definite but reverse aspect at the pole of mind. There they appear as passion, moods, emotion and feeling, in countless forms.

Inasmuch as emotion or feeling accompanies all display of energy, we conclude that it is a fixed characteristic of the energy, or rather the energy itself as seen from the mental side. Like all things in a world of polarity, energy exhibits both an internal and external aspect. The external aspect is the motion in matter which we refer to resident forces. The internal aspect is the emotion which follows the course of energy under the guidance of desire. Desire directs the energy. Feelings of pleasure and pain accompany its workings and its course.

2. The Quality of the Emotion Depends upon the Form of Energy Displayed.

Energy in its simplest form being a quantity proportional to the product of the mass of a body multiplied by the square of the velocity, it follows that with every variation in mass or velocity there will be a variation in the attendant emotion. The emotions that ordinarily reach consciousness, however, arise in a complex way. They are the product of energy in all forms of manifestation. In reverse expression, we find elements the equivalent of the volume and pressure of a head of water in hydraulics, of voltage and amperage in electrical science, and of tension and resistance in elastic bodies and solids. All physical elements with which we are familiar have appropriate expression, and the finer forces of nature intrude their equally subtle mental aspects. Out of this variety arise all emotions. Although they defy analysis until the physical counterpart is analyzed, neither creates the other; they support each other. They are opposite poles of the same thing.

Making allowance for the various forms in which energy works, the mental equivalent must be exactly as complex as the physical. A body quivering with emotion expresses at the mental pole the characteristics of the energy as it encounters varying conditions of resistance and conductivity. Driven by desire, energy is still amenable to law. It can work and spend itself only on the media at hand. Its quality must vary with each change in those media. Having gone forth as action, the energy will return as reaction. In reversing its course, the mental aspect also will change.

In a frenzy of emotion extremes are forced to a meeting point. This is why the acme of emotion along any line resolves itself into a reaction of satiety or dissolution.

Emotions such as anger or love, carried to the point of frenzy or rhapsody, suddenly find their limits and return upon themselves. The intensity of the action forces reaction. In this way the emotion may change almost instantly from courage to fear, from elation to melancholy. To be emotional is to move forth with the energy at one's command. It is to accelerate speed until the climax is reached and reaction and disgust, or death and extinguishment of that phase of one's experiences results.

The process is reversely similar to that which makes a seed germinate when planted in the warm, moist earth. Under seasonal changes, the form which conditions the life of the plant has reached its limit of contraction and condensation. It has stored in the seed potential energy to guide the creation of a new plant, but life cannot go further in that same direction. At the extreme of cold and death dissolution becomes the gateway to new life—embraces life. Polarity is asserted by bounding back to the other extreme of youth and intense life. In the rhythms of animal and plant life this meeting of extremes is clearly seen. As in ancient days, God moves upon the waters. The energy without quickens the energy within; the motion accelerates until the extreme is reached and death changes into life.

In art, literature, or physically in animal life, nothing creative is ever done save through emotion and this moving out toward death. Dissolution is the matrix in which the egg of genius is hatched. Thus it is that the man who would create a masterpiece must find some material sufficiently plastic and negative in which to work. He must dissolve, break up and destroy something in order to bring forth a new form. No great work was ever accomplished except through an emotion so overwhelming that it killed and destroyed. All things utilized in a masterpiece are first reduced to elemental essence, plastic and ready for reformation. Without this process the new, the original cannot appear.

If emotion enters into the creation of all masterpieces, it is also true that, once created, a work of art tends to awaken in others the same emotion. In what manner this is done we cannot explain here, although a few points need be borne in mind. One is that art expresses universal principles in concrete exemplifications. For this reason the attendant emotions are never discordant as long as the view is limited to the dominant idea expressed in the work of art. Another feature is that emotional participation in an observer is produced by an association and flow of ideas which inevitably enlarge his capacity for emotion. Although complete in itself, a work of art leads the mind on to the larger principles and laws back of the one expressed. As in geometry, all regular figures are but parts of more inclusive forms. The extended framework of musical composition is also an exemplication of this.

3. The Extremes of Emotion.

Between the extremes of emotion and the golden mean where polarity is forgotten in equilibrium are all degrees of feeling, graded in a sliding scale. This could not be otherwise, for some degree of emotion, or outmoving of energy, is essential to consciousness. Pure intellect is supposed to be motionless, calm, unmoved and cold; but even if such a condition can exist in a sentient being, we would still say that upon arriving at it all sense connection between subject and object had been lost. Emotion is a necessary element in all sensation, an ingredient of all polarized products. Its fires are maintained in every living, conscious individual. Its glow accompanies the course of all forces moving to and fro. Even the stable forms with which intellect deals seem products of a polarity so constant and of motion so infinitely rapid that activity becomes indistinguishable from rest.

Considering the genesis of emotion we have given, the

question arises as to how much emotion one should permit himself in the affairs of life. Should the dragon run rampant, tearing on continually toward an extreme of experience and death, or only when the idea and event is great enough to produce a masterpiece? Here intellect takes the bench and acts as judge. Otherwise an emotional individual is liable to become a breeder of monstrous progeny. Murder, wrath and lust in hideous forms are his children, while he himself, caught in a slough of despondency at time of reaction, is helpless and impotent. On the contrary, one with a fixed idea leading to the creation of the wonderful, the miraculous, proceeds to the limit of his power, even though reaction leads him to the negative pole of his being and death and decay results. He descends into hell (which here is defined as the satiety after intense emotion) in order that he may create a wonder and fascinate the world. But he who lets loose upon earth his emotional energy hap-hazard, defiantly caring nothing for results, is a terror both to himself and to humanity. He has no fixity of purpose, no firm resolve, no sense of sacrifice. Angry, he taunts and kills. Hungry, he steals and defrauds. Vile, he degrades and debauches. The difference between him and the true creator is not in the intensity of their passion, for in that they are the same, but in the firmness and fixedness of their ideas. One seeks chaos only; the other, through the gateway of chaos, finds cosmos.

The mild emotions of mankind are not productive of masterpieces; yet emotion is only a matter of degree. The processes of dissolution and rebirth perpetually attend it. Whether stormy or mild, whether acting in gentle or volcanic ways, its genesis is the same. It is a motion forth projectilely; a taking of object by subject through sensation. This may be done with the hands, the eyes, the ears, the nose or the mouth. The active storms the passive, captures, dissolves and makes of it a new thing. Emotion is the opposite of stagnation, quiescence and inertia, yet by the paradox of polarity, in reaction it returns to that very pole.

4. Active and Passive States of Emotion.

Inasmuch as reaction follows action and returns all energy to its source, it is manifest that emotion, being the mental equivalent of energy, will assume a different aspect as the direction of the energy is changed. From this change of course result two well defined states of activity and passivity. Outgoing energy produces positive or active emotions, returning energy the negative or passive. The intensity of these two classes of emotions may be equal, or graduated in any way so that a balance is finally struck. Although both the outgoing and returning currents are under the domination of will, and may be either accelerated or retarded, the aggregate amount of energy involved in the outflow and inflow of the tide is the same. In the end nothing is dissipated or lost. An enhanced intensity of experience only shortens the time over which it may extend. Slowly accumulated energy may force its way violently whenever the resisting power of the barriers is overmatched. The distinction between the two classes is of great importance. By understanding the outgoing wave one can regulate it. By knowing the inevitableness of its return one can endure what it brings. What is given forth slowly may be taken up rapidly. What has gone forth violently and impulsively, may be retaken and neutralized by patient care. By understanding this law of polarity, even sorrow is seen to support as its opposite, joy.

5. Abnormal Aspects of Emotion.

The conditions which surround the genesis and course of energy indicate with clearness what abnormal phases it may assume. Emotional excess of any kind may appear abnormal. A failure to show emotion at other times is equally abnormal. If bodily conditions are not properly developed for the storage and transmission of physical energy, irregular nervous and emotional reactions will result. This is already being recognized and studied more and more. Without normal inhibition of physical reflexes, emotional actions and reactions become exaggerated and interfere with the habits of ordinary life. Emotion without intellect is insanity.

In early stages of physical development, natural inertia prevents an undue display of emotional reactions beyond such as are intimately connected with the life and preservation of the species. As the physical body becomes a more facile conductor of energy, the intellect must step in to restore balance and order, or the fullness and excess of emotion tends to destroy the organized life which at first it tended to preserve.

One form of emotional response which is noticeable is mimicry and imitation. Most hysterical patients are at times excellent imitators. If an idea strikes them or they wish to describe something, the matter is produced with exaggerated pantomine. They seem to realize in sympathetic bodily form ideas which normal persons respond to sluggishly, if at all.

Emotion in some form accompanies all action and is the goal of desire, yet it is hardly an end in itself. He who would make it such is nearing the extinguishment of that particular desire.

CHAPTER V.

Pleasure and Pain.

1. Pleasure and Pain are Qualities attaching to all Emotions.

Pleasure and Pain are not things in themselves, but qualities which attach to something else. They are opposite qualities, and therefore must attach to the opposite poles of some process or thing. They appear in all emotion and therefore show that emotions are polarized products. Bearing in mind the fact that emotion accompanies all energy, let us analyze some of the more important processes of life and see what relation pleasure and pain bear to them.

Consciousness and unconsciousness are opposite states, being the poles of the most important rhythm of life. It is the same opposition as is found in the conceptions of life and death, sleeping and waking, light and dark, with the exception that it is more fundamental and absolute. In spite of this opposition, we still say that one pole implies the other. Like all polarized conceptions, you cannot define one element except on the background of the other. You cannot understand one until you understand the other. Each depends upon and supports the other. They are opposite poles of the same thing.

If, then, sleeping and waking, life and death, motion and rest are polarized aspects of one process, what relation do they bear to pleasure and pain? Does pleasure shine as a light eternal upon one pole and pain forever darken the other? Or is there some diurnal revolution and oscillation of the mathematical axis that at first gives to one pole the favored aspect and then bestows it upon the other? Which is the fixed element and what laws govern the adjustment of pleasure and pain to it?

Taking the matter as we find it, we conclude that pleasuse or pain is a quality which may attach to either pole. Polarity is a balanced, dynamic relation. It is established in motion and is maintained by self-adjustment. Its attributes are relative. In maintaining poise, any quality or aspect may disappear from one pole to reappear or be exhibited at the other. If the quality of pleasure or pain may attach to either pole, it is evident that it has something to do with balance or adjustment of the load. Polarized products are balanced products, yet at the same time complete balance results in quiescence and unconsciousness. In order that there may exist any consciousness or emotion there must take place an interchange of force between the poles. This interchange of force makes the poles conscious of each other, or, speaking more strictly, through consciousness it unifies the two poles and shows them to be opposite aspects of one thing. We conclude, therefore, that pleasure and pain depend upon the direction in which the energy is flowing with reference to the pole with which the consciousness at the time is identified.

2. Pleasure and Pain balance each other.

Far ahead in the perspective of the road of pleasure stalks the phantom of pain, ever in view. By pleasure we mean simply the sensation or feeling of being pleased. It is something we desire to continue. It is a sensational consciousness of gratifying desire. There is no element of completion in it. It is active, prospective and ever heading toward climax. Being in opposition to pain, it never loses sight of its inseparable mate. Possibly unclouded pleasure may be experienced by the extremely ignorant and non-self-conscious beings, who know nothing of reasoning and but little of experience, or by the more developed when under the sway of a new desire. A child will take a dancing delight in the flame of a fire until he gets too near to it and experiences the pain of a burn. Ever after, while he may still be charmed by the warmth and glow of the flame, his memory instructs him to be careful, and he anxiously bears the former experience in mind. Mingled with his delight is the old pain. We find no condition of pleasure, either in anticipation or realization, but has the other pole of pain dimly visible, both as a possibility and a probability, and that not far away. It could not be otherwise, seeing that pleasure consists in using the materials and forces within our environment in a reasonable manner. Departure of any kind from the limitations imposed at once injects into the experience the element of friction and pain. To restore the balance, energy must flow in the opposite direction, and that reversal of course of necessity changes the quality of the emotion.

From the foregoing it will be seen that pleasure and pain balance each other under the law of conservation of energy. Energy produces motion, motion assumes rhythmical form, and the forces that govern the vibrations and oscillations of the particles and masses of matter are constantly equalized as the motion progresses.

All strictly animal sense-pleasures are climaxed quickly and followed by reaction and satiety. To push the experience further in the same line would be followed by acute pain. As has been said, what is more distasteful than to eat when one is not hungry or to drink when one is not thirsty? Now the intellect anticipates all these things and sees the result in advance. No well developed self-conscious being indulges in wining and dining, or bestiality and voluptiousness, contributing nerve pleasure more or less ecstatic, without in the very act being overshadowed by the coming reaction and dreaded impotence and satiety. Even in the finer forms of sense-experience of the poet, artist or sculptor, beside his rapture and dream of ecstasy glides a nightmare figure ready later to spread its pall over the genius-creator and envelop him with sad disgust of his incomplete work and unfulfilled ideas. In the vulgar delights of the miser who clutches and hides moneys and jewels or accumulates property to gratify the mere sense of possession, there is the haunting image of the thief seeking his hiding place, or of the envious and hungry desiring his fortune. Anxiety tinctures all his pleasure. His deliberate acquisitiveness and furtive secretiveness, in the pain they produce, demonstrate the antithesis. Let a man love deeply a person or thing and he at once begins to worry about it. The deeper his attachment, the more gnawing is his anxiety. The more exquisite the pleasure of having and holding, the more exquisite is the pain at the prospect of losing. Houses, lands, monies, family, friends, clients, reputation, social status, personal attainments, physical and mental faculties, even ideals; anything in short that contributes to personal stature comes under this category.

Let an individual struggle to amass a fortune because the ease of wealth is bound to please. He reaches his goal and finds himself, perhaps, alone and companionless. He immediately searches for friendships, love and a home. This goal again reached, and himself pleased with congenial companionship, he discovers that in attaining the same his energy has been sapped. Nothing daunted, he starts out in pursuit of health, and finding it, discovers also that to keep the nice balance where he is poising with wealth, friends and health at hand, he must forever have his eye on his bank account, his heart attuned to his friends and a finger on his own pulse. Balancing thus, with old age not far off, disguised as pain, his pleasure is an anxious one, tremendously doubtful and alloyed.

As we before stated, no condition in life can be thought of where pleasure is pure and not tinctured with its other pole of pain, save that of irresponsible beings like infants and perhaps some animals. They too have their pain. although they may not bear it much in mind. Now what is this pain which mates pleasure so persistently? If pleasure is that which pleases a conscious individual, being a state which he desires to continue, pain is its opposite and must be that which he desires to cease. Pleasure is a co-ordinating, coherent, harmonious enjoyment of sensation and the attendant emotions in their high and low forms. Pain is an incoherent, chaotic, disrupting experience, the reverse of cosmic joy.

In all pleasure it is evident that, as the delight becomes intensified and accelerated when nearing its climax, it must at some point lose its co-ordination and pass from the unified cosmic condition to chaos. A picnic becomes a bacchanal, a holy feast an orgy. Knowing this, man must either let rhythm take its course, forcing him on to the climax of pleasure to dash him later head downward into the burning chaos of pain and the disgusting quagmire of satiety, or he must cut short his pleasures before completion, substituting, thereby, another form of pain for that to which the climax of the rhythm would lead him. If he has an appetite for food, he may experience pleasure in it and stop short before he has gorged himself. The uncompleted desire is a different pain from that of revulsion of feeling and satiety, but he cannot divorce pleasure from pain, nor pain from pleasure. They are opposite poles of the same thing and exactly balance.

3. Polarity and Cross-Polarity.

We stated in the preceding paragraph that pleasure uses the materials and forces within our environment in a reasonable manner and that a departure of any kind from the limitations imposed injects into the experience the elements of friction and pain. We also call attention to the fact that harmonious action repeated over and over results in a constantly diminishing consciousness. The being that maintains full consciousness forever encounters discordant elements and friction. To live, he must organize and conquer chaos. To meet it supinely is to be swallowed up in its darkness. To rest in the harmony produced by the efforts of others is to enter the lethal river of forgetfulness and sleep.

From the foregoing we see that discord produces pain and harmony pleasure. We have re-defined the question but encounter the same polarity, for there is no harmony without discord, nor discord without harmony. Each defines and supports the other. They are opposite poles of the same thing. Finding polarity in all our concepts, we look farther to discover whether or not there is cross-polarity, or polarity of higher power or degree. It at once becomes evident that this is the case. Back of every polarized product stands the unifying process that created it. The poles stand apart only as we identify ourselves with one and face the other. Rising to a point of view that embraces both poles, a higher polarity is encountered. It is cross-polarity and at right angles to the space occupied by the first product. As in space of three dimensions the unity pervading space of two dimensions is seen, so by comprehending a polarized concept of higher power, the lower concept and creation depending upon it is immediately comprehended and seen. Through this door lies the escape from both pleasure and pain. Under the illumination afforded, it is seen that pleasure for one creature is always pain for another, but by operation of the great law, action equals reaction and the tide must reverse itself. In the long run neither will remain indebted to the other. Desire is an eternal search for and finding of pleasure. Anything desired is pleasurable. The gratifying of desire is pleasurable. But a desire gratified is a desire annihilated. The outgoing energy has reached its limit; its returning current must display the opposite mathematical sign. But for him who stands above there is neither pleasure nor pain. It is only life. He would not reduce it to nothingness by taking from it the pleasure and the pain.

4. The Physical Basis of Pleasure and Pain.

Recent biological investigations establish the fact that consciousness in the. animal organism tends to reside in the organ last formed or evolved. According to this conception, the organ which is in the most unstable condition and most called upon to adapt itself to changing environment is the chief seat of consciousness. If, from the viewpoint of the physical body, consciousness resides in the brain, it must not be forgotten that it is only the functions the brain is called upon to perform that make it the seat of consciousness. When there was no brain or when the brain was not developed to its present importance, there were other organs that shared the honor of holding the attention of the Unit of Force and of forming the field of its consciousness.

It is reasonable to conclude that every organ as formed monopolized much of the consciousness of the individual and that only after the organ had reached a comparatively stable state of conformity to environment did consciousness leave it to operate automatically. This reduction of conscious processes to automatic processes is constantly going on. It is not confined to any organ or to any particular portion of the body. Processes which at first require attention and effort, as soon as the habit is set, become automatic. Full consciousness no longer lingers there. The law of economy of energy and parsimony of effort prevails. Habit and automatic action replace whenever possible voluntary processes, leaving consciousness free to undertake other tasks.

If it be true that consciousness has shed its light at one time or another on every portion of the evolving organism, it is also true that the organ or evolved structure when left to function automatically has not been wholly expelled from the field of consciousness of the Unit. It still stands within its field of force and may come into consciousness of its own motion or by voluntary effort of the Unit. Ordinary consciousness can pick up the local consciousness of almost any portion of the body and a trained and concentrated consciousness seems able to penetrate any realm. Like all natural processes the extent to which this is possible depends upon the amount of energy at command and the knowledge and skill with which it is directed.

Considering, then, that consciousness has resided at one time or another in every portion of the body, and that it may now voluntarily return to any portion towards which it is properly directed, also that it may be attracted to any tissue that experiences pleasure or pain of sufficient intensity, we have a reasonable physical basis for understanding pleasure and pain.

The law that comes out of this state of facts is this: Consciousness at the present stage of evolution is pressing upward to reach a physical height from which it can gather richer experiences and dominate larger processes. In doing this, it gradually reduces to subordinate, automatic action all organic processes from which it can safely withdraw the attention. Consciousness, however, is niggardly of effort and avoids unnecessary expenditure of energy. It is a loss for it to retread the ground over which it has already passed. The inertia and shock of giving up a matter already in consciousness is painful. The withdrawal and transfer of attention to a disturbed portion of the body takes energy and is an interference with the higher tasks mapped out for consciousness. Physical pain, as does all pain, arises from the disturbance of harmonic processes and relations. The pain which is directly caused by the disturbed local condition is aggravated by the disturbance that the higher consciousness inevitably feels. But the secret of the whole matter is the loss of energy devoted to other purposes. All disturbed processes absorb energy, and energy, the only servant of desire, can be ill spared. Physical pain, then, we would define as the shock, resistance and loss felt by the Unit of Force upon giving up energy to meet the needs of a disturbed organ or automatic process in the body over which it rules.

5. Abnormal Aspects of Pleasure and Pain.

Pleasure generally takes the initiative in the events of life, and pain follows the climax. Sometimes this order is reversed. With some, pleasure and pain are so fully together in consciousness that they can hardly call their higher experiences either pleasure or pain. One of the marks of genius is this peculiar melancholy. The genius, in fullness of consciousness, sees with awful distinctness the shadow embracing his pleasure, even to its death.

Ordinary men are not so clear sighted. But the genius is not ordinary; therefore he is melancholy in his raptures and sombre in his ecstacies.

Pleasure and pain, in one sense, are the product of a struggle between chaos and cosmos. The tendency towards dissolution and an unorganized condition is at times just as strong as the tendency towards an evolved and cosmic condition. Either condition too long indulged produces an effort to restore the equilibrium. Inertia characterizes both aspects. A body in motion manifests its inertia as well as one at rest. If, by intense or too long indulged experiences a great departure from equilibrium has been made, the effort towards readjustment involves a mighty struggle, setting up in consciousness a very hell of abnormal experience which is termed pain. As bitter as pain seems in the bearing, it has a sweetness at its heart. Like pleasure, it is ever conscious of its antithesis or other pole and strives continually for balance and equilibrium between the two. The sufferer is but taking good and wholesome medicine if he but understands the rhythm in the experiences of his outraged senses. In the cradle of experience man rocks back and forth between the poles of his being, between pleasure and pain.

CHAPTER VI.

Imagery.

1. Imagery is Consciousness of Form and Motion.

By imagery we mean consciousness of form and motion. Inasmuch as Units of Force co-exist, the perception or recognition of this co-existence gives form; and inasmuch as the relations between them change, the perception of this change appears as motion and as qualitative and quantitative differences. Imagery, then, begins as simple sensation, showing time and space elements, and persists with modifications through percept, concept and abstract thinking until it is dissolved in a direct intuition of the ultimate form of existence. By this dissolution, however, it is immediately thrown back upon concrete exemplification and particular sensations and images.

From this we see that imagery is but the power of the Unit to realize its relations in time and space, a necessary product of polarity and rhythm. Being included in consciousness, and a part of consciousness, imagery has the same expansions and contractions as consciousness. Images come and go and their apparent size and distinctness vary. The qualities that characterize them do not remain constant or fixed. This, as we have said before, is a result of the change in relation between Units of Force.

Imagery, as we here use the term, is the concrete content of consciousness. It includes all sensation, that is to say, all that arises in consciousness under the form of space and time. It applies equally well to the product of any of the senses. By our hypothesis, it applies also to the product of any senses hitherto possessed or that shall hereafter be evolved. It is existence sensed and perceived, our only means of knowing concrete reality. It is the form assumed in knowledge of the contact and interdealing of Units of Force, the essence and ultimate nature of things in themselves expressed in specialization. This being the case, it is meaningless to assign higher rank or reality to one sensation or image than to another. It makes no difference whether they arise within or without, voluntarily or involuntarily, as apparent facts or as conscious fancies. Imagery, wherever it appears, is a form that existence has assumed, does assume and will assume, and as such is a recorded fact forever.

This necessary conclusion regarding the nature of imagery is in no way inconsistent with the distinctions we draw between practical, every-day facts and imagination and illusions. These distinctions, so important in themselves, depend upon the organs through which we receive sensations and through which we can affect and be affected by the outer world. Consciousness, therefore, when confined to physical organs, assigns to all imagery a value and rank in accordance with its ability to stimulate and answer to the physical senses. The limitations are in the organs themselves and are gradually removed as the organs evolve greater capacity, or as new organs answer to a special environment.

The power to conjure mental images is indispensible to consciousness. We think through the relativity and concatenation of images. No thought is possible without a series of symbols. We sometimes speak of a person as without imagination, but by our hypothesis all self-conscious individuals must have imagery in a greater or less degree.

Imagery, then, is an attribute of self-conscious mind, wherever found. We do not need to go into an argument to demonstrate this fact. Any person can prove it to himself by attempting to think without images, and to convey that thought to another, or even fully to understand himself. A vague consciousness might be conjectured as possible when one closes his eyes and shuts out objectivity at the same time vetoing picture-making within. Any alertness, force or coherency, expressed interiorly or exteriorly, will in spite of himself take form, and form is imagery, the father of the idea, the mother of the thought.

When the earth was without form and void, it was without thought or idea, if such a condition is conceivable. The capacity to form a shape and individualize an idea is inherent in mind. Imagery and idea are the texture of mind, even memory is but a structure of form and shapes attached infallibly to a perspective which implies time, space and specialization. A future outlook, also, is never divorced from form and image and therefore is eternally mated with time, space, perspective and particulars. It would seem as if nothing is formless save law, and law therefore is the unthinkable abstraction, which, while it is, is yet by the nature of its shapelessness unknowable, until it expresses itself in form.

Having discovered, by self evidence, that form and idea are necessary to thought, and therefore in all thinking creatures, we also conclude there is a difference in the power of imagery in the various genera that we know. Taking man as capable of the highest expression of language or symbol making, we find that he is at the acme of power in that respect. His spoken words inadequately express the intensity of his imagination. An impediment in speech or timidity, will prevent him from orally expressing even as far as possible the rich world of ideas within his brain. Sometimes he will strive in writing or picture-drawing to tell the tales of mind that his tongue refuses to reveal. Sometimes, again, he will not bring forth anything at all, only showing by the expression of his face the whirlpool of seething thought and imagery within his fiery mind. Although there is this abundance of imagery within the mind, unexpressed and incapable of full expression, there is a strong and ever-present tendency to externalize it and give it expression. This is the significance of language, its purpose and function being a constant mediation between the outer and the inner world. Facing both ways, it partakes of the characteristics of both. Being an externalization of thought, all language depends upon images and symbols. We have them in the form of letters, which we put together and make into image words. We have them in hieroglyphics and in all devices which condense an idea into a Unit. In concrete form they loom up before our interior eye, and in their suggestiveness become a story condensed or a narrative close-packed. Whether we use language in speaking to ourselves or others, it consists of letters, words, images, hieroglyphics or symbols, beaded together and compacted to express ideas and establish relations. Any being that can think must have the gift of imagery.

We have here spoken of the imagery of self-conscious beings and the relation it bears to thought and language; but there is a larger aspect of the matter, which, under our hypothesis, we cannot ignore. We refer to the form and imagery that permeates all nature, the struggle between the geometrical shapes of crystallization, the spheroidal shapes of cell life, and the curved lines of all motion. In this sense we know of no chaos that is not shaped by form and that does not inevitably establish within itself internal relations and imagery. As we said in the early part of this book, consciousness is implied in the motion of all particles of matter, and for that reason, the structure of all chemical elements, the forms of all plant and animal life, the shapes assumed by every thing and creature, however far they fall short of our standard of self-consciousness, are, nevertheless, the imagery of some mind, the joy and fulness of some life and consciousness.

2. Space and Time Elements in Imagery.

All imagery is presented to us in a setting of space and time, and with varying perspective. It makes no difference whether we consider space and time as an inherent part of external nature, or whether we consider them as forms which the mind imposes on the content of consciousness. By our hypothesis, mind and matter are opposite poles of the same thing, and, therefore, all that appears necessary, a priori, in the mind will also appear as a uniform principle or law in the external world. Likewise, space and time can be studied equally well from either pole. Externally, we reduce all to geometry and mathematics. Internally, we discover the unity which binds together both space and time and which appears as an inner form or neccssity, so that in one sense thinking is both dependent upon and independent of space and time. Whichever view is taken, it is certain there is no attribute of either space or time, but which will be reversed at the other pole of being. By this means a new light can be thrown upon any perplexing situation into which inquiry may lead us.

Considering imagery as conditioned by space and time, in the sense above explained, it is evident that it is merely a portion of experience presented to us like any other phenomenon in space and time. Even in its most evanescent and subtle form, it is not distinguishable from every day facts, except by such distinctions as we draw between one fact and another. It cannot arise uncaused nor does it disappear without cause. Its nearness in space and time, and its intensity and varying qualities, depend upon the energy poured into some mould of form created by relations between Units of Force. Wherever energy operates, there is cause and effect. Energy is required either to produce or perceive imagery, therefore all imagery is the effect of some cause and in turn the cause of some effect.

3. Form and Motion are Antithetical Concepts.

In the preceding paragraphs we have seen how imagery is subject to space, time and causality, and whether we treat these concepts as external principles or as inner forms of the mind, the practical result is the same. Imagery is a fact of consciousness, and, although developed in all degrees of intensity and with varying perspective, it is never disassociated from external phenomena and is subject to the same laws. It is consciousness of form and motion, and therefore a primal product of all interdealing between Units of Force.

If imagery is consciousness of form and motion, it seems also true that this consciousness of form and motion is the only content of consciousness. Although necessary elements in consciousness, form and motion are nevertheless antithetical concepts, being consistently opposed to each other as poles of one process or thing. The paradox of motion and rest is very old in philosophy and one of the most difficult to treat, yet it is at the foundation of all our ideas regarding space and time. Connect these concepts with the idea of substance, and there is drawn in the further problem of cause and effect. Treating of psychological facts, under our hypothesis, we conclude that these antithetical concepts are not self-cancelling. They are change-concepts in which either element may be substituted for the other. If one element is considered as rest, the other is motion. If what was conceived of as in motion be treated as the element of rest, the other element preserves the same relations, but appears as motion. Thus it is that motion and rest are polarized aspects of one process and together produce an evolving, living thing.

Applying these distinctions to imagery, we see that form is but a specialization of space relations concealing in itself the element of motion or change. We treat it as the stable element in our sense experience, and yet it vanishes from our gaze and consciousness, for we have unwittingly shifted to the other pole of being and permitted it to escape as motion. Having this element as its other aspect, it must manifest it whenever through energy there is set in motion the rhythmic swing of cause and effect.

4. Sensation is the Physical Recognition of Form and Motion.

The physical recognition of form and motion appears as sensation, and, has in it the potentiality of imagery in all higher and subtler forms. As sense organs are gradually evolved, the character of sensations received from the same stimuli varies greatly, or at least there is a selecting and ignoring out of the complexly presented stimulus which amounts to the same thing. The eye that has no recognition of certain colors today, may in time add to its sensations what seems an entirely new experience, although proved to be a response to higher vibrations of the class previously sensed. Even in the lifetime of the individual the efficiency of the sense organ may vary greatly.

Along with the fact that our sense organs evolve so as to bring into consciousness things previously ignored, we also bear in mind that they drop from consciousness matters for which they have no further use. This selective attention, by our hypothesis, inheres in all matter, and, directed from the mental pole of the unit, gives to natural processes a form of purposiveness so often thought to be explained. As to why this appears in consciousness as physical sensation, we say that motion results from energy interchanged between Units of Force, and the change of relations in the physical body thus affected is, at the mental pole, sensation.

5. Abnormal Aspects of Imagery.

If a man is a thinker and has ideas, he is bound to have images of them whether outwardly manifested or not. Confined within his compact skull he will find a world of chaos, where the forms and shapes crowd and jostle in their struggle for expression. Often the imagination overpowers the mind that has bred it, and he becomes incoherent or insane. In the majority of cases, however, imagery finds some way out of the head and hits exterior conditions. Ideas take wings and fly from star to star. Our imaginations are wanderers straying over the universe formed and terrible. Man conceives an idea, and this nucleus takes shape and individuality, until it exteriorizes itself in a machine, a picture, a speech, a poem, a statue, or a song, and becomes visible to its parent in matter, yet the visible, material expression is never the pure idea which is still so terribly alive in invisibility that the whole universality of being is more or less under its sway.

Perhaps we should not have said that man—a man—can conceive this idea at all. Undoubtedly in some subtle way it has always existed vaguely shaped and indestructible. But man seems to have the power to intensify its expression through his imagination, and to all intents and purposes as far as he is concerned, it becomes his own creation. All conceivable images are latent or possible in the universal mind. Sentient beings, however, revivify them, making them dynamic and stupendous. A highly imaginative race is generally great, either for evil or good. The same may be asserted of a highly imaginative individual. If his power of imagery is great, and his means of expression small, through faulty technic, or a physical impediment, his overcrowded ideas lack coherence, and the man becomes a menace to the world. Such a person is liable to be a mischief maker, a crank or a maniac. On the other hand, if his imagination has a clear channel for expression so that the head and brain are not congested, coherence and order result, his ideas going forth winged and golden.

Coherence and incoherence make a clearly defined difference between rationality and irrationality. If a man has what is called "a poor imagination," he may, nevertheless, through a talent of ready expression and a backing of great force, make his few ideas "tell" with more accurate certainty than can the richer mind less dynamic in energy.

Image-making is a source of both delight and terror, a fountain inexhaustible. How it is possible to conjure images we do not know. The law of its working, however, is quite easy to discover, and one of the objects of psychology is to make it plain. Pictures are "called up," but the depth of the abyss of apparent nothingness from which they come it is impossible to sound. Nevertheless the mind desires and they appear, sometimes without our so willing. An individual is flooded with them much to his dismay and then his "mind wanders"—people declare. They discern in the imagination something dreadful to contemplate. What is a haunted house in horror compared with a haunted mind? Ideas intrude themselves and active, tumble about recklessly, the vicious and angelic in each others' arms, beauty and ugliness cheek to cheek, the grotesque and the sublime lip to lip. The brain has become a place of obscene debauchery, where a bacchanal in full swing has put down and out all sense of fitness, order and sequence. The will of the father of this chaos is unequal to the subduing of his children. Like Saturn, he is forced to devour them, and becomes a mental dyspeptic and terror to mankind. Vice versa—who is so blessed as he who has a sane and powerful imagination? Poor and alone, yet he needs no pity, for his world is peopled and beautiful—indeed, he is richer than the poverty-brained millionaire who tries to buy his way to happiness with coin alone. Alladin and his wonderful lamp are symbols of this man of rich imagination. Into the world of his inner life leaps full-armed the Minerva of his desire. Down from high Olympus she travels golden-sandaled, carrying messages from the mountain of Zeus. Back she flies to the King and Lord, bearing in her arms his full-formed creations cut in earth and chiseled in stone. So to be a great, coherent image maker is to be a God.

As all conceivable form and forms are in the bosom of the universal, and as the word "conjure" means nothing new save as we have forgot, then it makes no difference whether the fruit of the imagination is something we have seen objectively in matter or something apparently new to our consciousness. The result is imagery, nevertheless; and in its last analysis is not creative, but is made to manifest with emphasis, deluding us in our forgetfulness into thinking that it is an absolutely new idea.

CHAPTER VII.

Memory and Imagination.

1. Memory and Imagination are Specializations of Imagery.

It is evident that all sensations and mental imagery are in one sense a present experience of the individual. They are a part of the NOW of consciousness as much as anything else that fills it, although we recognize that many of the images do not have immediate importance. Unconsciously we separate the images of the stream of thought into classes. There are those that have to do with the immediate contact of external reality, those which appertain to a recognized portion of our experiences, those which represent and forecast some experience to be, and those which we handle in imagination without certainty as to whether a more definite use of them is to follow. The distinction we are here pointing out is, that there is a faculty which divides imagery into these kinds. It not only assigns to the image a position in the stream of time, but also has to do with the degrees of externality and intensity which characterize the imagery. As we said before, all imagery has its source in contact and inter-dealing between units of force. In this chapter, therefore, we shall treat only of the specialized forms of imagery known as memory and imagination.

Memory can never be considered apart from the image-making power, because the very nature of memory is that of a series of images recalled. The mind is continually taking photographs of passing events which it files away to be recollected on proper occasions, and marshalled to the front to be scanned by interior eyes. The continuity of the mind's experiences is its memory made manifest through images, and these images which constitute the symbols of its past acts, emotions and thoughts, generally fall together in groups which we call the association of ideas. Call up a face from the abyss of other years, and around it will gather a habitation and its occupants. It is almost impossible to get a past experience isolated. Near it will cluster other and still other experiences related to it until a spiral of images will coil upon itself, electric with sensation and dynamic with life. Through our power of image-making and of retaining the same we revivify old emotions, actually forcing the past into the present, blotting out for the time being the local environment and substituting in its place another seemingly long gone.

The best understanding of memory can be obtained through our power to forget. Memory has been quaintly defined as the thing we forget with. This forgetting is a full half of memory; or putting it another way, the bringing into consciousness and expelling from consciousness the images of past experiences is the process called memory. This process is at times voluntary, and at other times involuntary. The images may appear creatures of our will, and again they seem to possess life and to impose themselves on us by their own energy. Be this as it may, it is certain that forgetting is an essential half of the process. Without it the past would stand before us condensed and rigid. The plethora of images would be intolerable and meaningless.

We doubt if man could retain life an hour under the pressure of complete consciousness in memory. Through forgetfulness, however, he breathes, thinks and grows, blotting out in a sense the visions of other days, suffering them to return in single file, or in limited numbers to nourish the mental life of the moment.

From the foregoing we see that the images of memory are specialized. They have to do with the past. They are held in a perspective which gives to us a past. This recognition and personal perspective, however, is not the only specialization that characterizes them. The fact that they return to consciousness differentiates them from other images. Out of all the past few images are permitted much return. This return is a purposive process, a specialization in itself. The Unit of Force wills and desires and undertakes certain purposes. Out of the past come only the images that are attracted to these by the energy remaining in them and originally contributed to them by the Unit of Force. Through this energy they attach to the Unit as memories. It is impossible to be mindful of that upon which one has not expended himself. Only those experiences which have absorbed a portion of one's energy can remain and cluster around him, seeking at all favorable rhythms of mental life to restore to him his own. With this view of memory, the element of personal recognition is explained. Memories are memory because they hold in suspension a portion of the energy contributed to the original event. They come and go both as I call and as they will because we are bound together by indissoluble magnetism. The suspension in memory is but a part of that holding both together and apart which constitutes creation. As there is nothing created without energy, so with memory—its vividness, its intensity, its emotions, the recognition that inheres in it, all depend upon this virtue that has gone out of the individual. As we have seen before, by the law of rhythm all energy returns undiminished to its source. Until then, the Grand Cycle of experiences to which memories attach cannot be closed.

2. The Element of Perspective in Memory and Imagination.

In the preceding paragraph we have shown how personal recognition in memory depends upon the energy originally contributed to the remembered event by the individual remembering. This energy makes the image inevitably his and a part of his past. The same principle applies to the imagery of imagination. Imagination is a specialized form of imagery, because the individual contributes to it energy. Image making, in all degrees of intensity, is a power possessed by the Unit of Force.

To make images, however, he must use energy, and the fact that he has used energy in the creation of the images at once transforms them into a part of his memory and subjects them to memory's laws. This relation between imagination and memory is seldom noted, but its importance is apparent. Sensations, perceptions and imaginations, when once born in consciousness, are immediately converted into memories. They and the emotions that accompany them are the content of consciousness.

Having come to the conclusion that all energy by the law of action and reaction is attached to the individual that gives it forth, and that it is this inevitable magnetism that makes the images created by it a recognizable part of one's past, the inquiry remains as to how the perspective of the past is maintained in memory. This perspective, we conclude, is established in two ways. First, by the amount of energy inhering in the image. Second, by location in the series of rhythms through association of ideas. With reference to the first law, we find that time tends to draw from mental images their vitality. Every time a remembered image is called up, a devitalization takes place, unless for special reasons the Unit pours into the mould of the image new energy. As a consequence, memories of even the most vivid events gradually cease to interest and lose importance. The adjustments necessitated have been largely made and the energy of the original experience to that extent returned and compensated. If, however, some new crisis in life arises wherein this older event becomes important, the magnetism between the old and the new becomes apparent. Similars tend to coalesce. Like seeks like, although supported by its opposite. In clusters of this kind memories seem best to lodge. Magnetic attraction in the physical world, under our hypothesis, would be association of ideas at the mental pole, and equally valuable as an explanation of the phenomena involved.

From the foregoing it follows that the perspective of memory is not definite and clear like the perspective of space. A remembered event may be quickly sapped of its vitality and lose position in mental perspective, while another may linger longer with comparatively little loss of energy. Along with this, must be borne in mind the fact that the Unit can impart to the images new vitality, and prolong their lease of life. The perspective, therefore, that arises from the amount of energy retained by the image is uncertain and deceptive. It is like a room in which lights are raised and lowered, causing the walls apparently to advance and recede.

The truer perspective of memory is established by rhythm. Under the analysis of memory here given, it will be seen that time resolves itself into a series of rhythms in which the Unit of Force participates. Without these rhythms, for the Unit there would be no time. The time given us by rhythm, however, is all that heart could wish. In spite of the untimed complexity of each event, there mounts above the moments in which it has its climax the mighty rhythms of days, weeks, lunar months, seasons, years, equinoctial precessions and cosmic cycles, in each of which the Unit of necessity participates and spends itself. Without this causal participation, history would have no meaning, and the geologic past would be without charm. Leaving in its wake a portion of itself, the self finds this wonderful framework to support its memories, both the actual and potential, to make them comprehensible and to give them meaning.

If rhythm gives perspective to memory, it also affords the architectural framework of the future. Prospective imagination may anticipate the course of a rhythm, and in the eye of the mind behold the images of events to be. The prevision and swift moving of the mind in this regard is also subject to the laws of energy. Again and again we see difficulties facing us, but the images are too feeble to attract full attention and give us the courage to act. As with the past, it is easy to see with distorted perspective and obscured vision. The undeveloped mind holds consciously little of the future in its grasp and draws but few lessons from the past.

3. Variations in Intensity of Memory and Imagination.

In the last paragraph it was suggested that the Unit of Force could pour into the mould of a mental image new energy or in due course withdraw from the image the vitality already possessed. By our hypothesis, this would affect the vividness and intensity of the image and determine the amount of attraction and repulsion between one image and another and between past images and current events. This attraction and repulsion is at the base of association of ideas and suggests the law by which memories enter and depart from the mind. The vibrations which result in consciousness are set upon a sliding scale. As the image is drawn nearer or retreats the rate of vibration is relatively increased or diminished, and this affects the vividness and associational qualities of the image.

We here make a distinction between the imagery of memory or imagination, upon which the Unit spends energy directly, and images that come and go in consciousness as though they were sensations appealing directly to some interior sense. These latter images, once perceived, pass into the reservoir of memory and may also form the content of imaginative creations. In their inception, they do not arise out of either memory or imagination in the ordinary sense. By our hypothesis, however, they are matter of some grade set in motion by energy and, therefore, sensations of a subtler form.

The intensity of memory and imagination are independent of the character or form of the imagery. Sense organs are set to respond to vibrations of certain rates, but in addition to this the element of intensity enters into the sensations. A musical instrument may be struck so as to produce the same note, first scarcely audible and then so loud as to be painful. The pitch of the tone is determined by the vibration rate or limitations in the vibrating part of the instrument, but its intensity depends upon the amount of energy transferred to it by the percussion producing the musical note. It is the same with imagery. All events seem to be contained in a spiral roll of the past. They pertain directly to all persons in proportion to the energy contributed by each to produce them. Being facts and events they have a settled and indestructible form. Unless supported by new energy they become devitalized and contract to such fineness as to pass unnoticed. Having a fixed rate of vibration imposed upon them by their form, they of necessity have their affinities and associational counterparts in the countless tones and overtones of mental life. The result of this is that an intense mental note struck at any time will awaken countless memories lying concealed beneath the threshold of consciousness. Not only this, but as the spiral of life coils upon and over itself it draws near many past events that had been lying too distant to attract attention. The new nearness, however, is sufficient to bring them within the magnetic field of the mind and they at these favorable moments reach consciousness and contribute their part to the varied and ever shifting imagery of the mind.

From the foregoing it would seem that all events retain their form or shape but vary in what might be called importance or size. Once past, they tend to "go down fine" and drop below the threshold of consciousness. It is energy and only energy that can keep them expanded and hold them as present and important facts of the mind. When they depart from consciousness, however, they are not dead, but reduced in vitality. As they recede in the perspective of time, they become smaller. By their distance they escape more and more from the field of consciousness dominated by the Unit of Force. Let occasion arise, however, either by favorable position in what we must call the spiral of life, or by any intense experience and need of the mind which sends far and near a cry for sympathy and understanding, and they may be awakened. By the new energy radiating to them they may be restored even to the fullness and vividness of the original event.

Under the law of energy above explained, and by our hypothesis, it follows that one may consciously seek out an event or experience held in the mind and deliberately pour into it energy so as to make it pleasurable or painful in the old way and full of instruction. Likewise the imaginative creations of the mind may be given an intensity that becomes a creative principle, a part of the very process, evolution and life of nature itself. Without doubt all imaginations, being matter of some grade set in motion by energy, do contribute to all processes of growth and life, although we may be but little aware of it. In this connection we would call attention to a distinction between memory and imagination. The images of memory are all in the receding wave of some rhythm. The energy is departing from them. The height of the wave is lowering and seeking rest. With imagination the opposite is the case. Energy is being poured directly into all imaginative creations. We imagine things in which we participate either with pleasure or with a desire to avoid. They are creations of our wills and desires. They form the ideals we desire to realize in the most substantial manner possible. Always on the crest of an advancing wave, imaginations are a part of the mighty energy that moves and supports the world.

When we say a man forgets, we do not imply that he has lost an iota of his former life. Somewhere involved within him is all that he has experienced, but he recollects it only as consciousness will permit. Consciousness in this matter is a stern dictator, and allows man to remember but a few experiences at any one time. There are some exceptions known to this, such as that awful experience when one is in great peril or danger of sudden death. Then the flood gates of memory open and **all that has been** overwhelms the soul in consciousness.

As a rule, however, the tendency of mind is to concentrate on specializations and nothing short of the most deadly excitation of the nerves has power temporarily to change this attitude. While in consciousness we get memories in localized images, grouped through the law of association, yet in reality the **sui generis** and detached aspects in which these groups appear are indicative of a complete chain of memories, that, though lying just beyond consciousness, are, nevertheless, there.

In sequence under the law of cause and effect there is no hiatus possible. If one thing is to be recorded on the tablet of mind all things that mind has experienced are recorded also. Not the smallest sensation in the chain of events is omitted. The apparent hiatus—the apparent vacuum—is in consciousness only, and that accounts for the fact of recollection or the power of calling up images supposedly not existent, and facts apparently entirely forgotten. This hiatus in consciousness, this ability to forget, is best proof of the exactness and eternity of memory. Out of the universe of things and experiences nothing is ever lost. In the realm of the emotions and ideas, which realm by the law of memory is eternally preserved according to normal sequence, this law holds good. Now the realm of emotions and ideas is mind—mind universal and mind particular. An individual's mind, then, can know nothing of a hiatus in actuality. Preserved there are all experiences of his life intact, not one missing, nor by the exactness of cause and effect can they ever escape. The events that go to make up his experiences are linked in a chain indestructibly. By no possibility can this individual chain, his chain—differing by the law of his individuality and environment from that of every other being—be destroyed or annihilated. No two things can possibly be alike in the universe, for, although as seemingly paired as well-matched twins, the very fact that they cannot occupy the same place at the same time makes them different in environment and point of view and, therefore, in themselves no two chains of memory can be the same. Consequently, as nothing can ever be lost, these chains of memory by nature differing one from the other, are eternal. This argument, of course, is based on the accepted axioms that nothing is ever lost and that no two things can occupy the same place at the same time.

Look back in the past in your memory anywhere and try to detach cause from effects, or associated ideas from one another,—it cannot be done. The images which symbolize them are eternal. To be sure they drop out of consciousness, but only out of consciousness, never out of the realm of ideas. By no possibility can anything in the universe be annihilated or destroyed. And this proves individual persistence of particular chains of memory and therefore eternal persistence of individual existence. Admitting the law of causality, the power to image events and experiences through sequence, the impossibility of a hiatus in the chain of cause and effect, the particularism attached to time and space, and therefore events, the certainity that nothing can be lost—not even a mental concept—and we establish through memory and the personalism thereto attached an eternity of individual beings, sometimes awake, again asleep, but everlastingly persistent and indestructible.

When man forgets, he sleeps; when he remembers, he is awake. By our hypothesis of polarity, waking and sleeping are opposite conditions in consciousness or unconsciousness. As either state cannot be maintained indefinitely, man balances eternally near one or the other pole. When an individual awakes after a night of approximate unconsciousness, he picks up the thread of memory where he dropped it and adds on to it the period of unconsciousness through which he has just passed, treating it as an experience and giving it a place in the series of events. That this period of apparent unconsciousness may contain other experiences recognizable by a higher power of consciousness, is not only probable, but under our hypothesis, necessary. The Unit of Force is never without contact with matter in motion and therefore with consciousness pitched at some octave in the scale of being.

Without memory, man could neither think nor live,

as we understand life. Without memory, an eternity of individuality, the consciousness of a past and the prospect of a future would alike be inconceivable. By memory in its broadest sense, we mean not only the exclusive consciousness of things gone, but the chain of events intact which is lost only in the seeming. Nothing is ever lost. And here is apparent the meaning of that misunderstood term "recognition." A man seems to have absolutely forgotten something or some one, seen perhaps in early youth, but let him be brought face to face with the object, and, if not suddenly, after a time there will steal over him the consciousness of familiarity, culminating later in complete recognition. In his mind somewhere, though apparently gone forever, was the response to the thing recalled. Some bead in his chain of memories was the image of the object presented to his gaze. Upon imaging the present object, perhaps much changed, by the law of association of ideas and parsimony of mental storage room, the old and the new are drawn to each other and coalesce.

To be able to forget or remember at will implies great power of concentration, for it means nothing other than the fixing of the mind so intently upon some specialization that all things outside it are eliminated from consciousness. By expelling the disturbing present, images of the far past may be made to appear. The man who willfully forgets, is the man who concentrates. Such a person, when he chooses, remembers with more distinctness than ordinary individuals, for upon any experience gone through with he can concentrate also. Therefore when the time comes the good forgetter is intense in recollection. His energy in both domains is at his command. Through practice he realizes that remembering and forgetting are opposite poles of the same process or thing.

In old age the mind is so filled with data and generalizes to such a degree that it seems impossible to fix attention upon any one thing. The old person finds it hard to remember, yet seems never entirely to forget. He dwells in thought largely in the past, upon experiences long gone, but scarcely with an intense memory. Instead, he seems to be watching the scenes of other days with the eye of an observer, rather than entering into them with the true zest of one who remembers emotionally, recalling his angers, hates and passions, and living them over again. Having ceased to live vividly in the present and no longer filling it with intense and all absorbing thoughts, the imagery of the past is not held at a distance, but drifts in upon him by its natural and inevitable attraction. Little vitality is needed to enable an image momentarily to fill a place in his memory. The whole process is a natural part of the closing rhythm of life. Having lost interest in the activities of the present, he works over and over the past, each time drawing in to himself some of its substance, until nowhere is left a current of energy sufficient to awaken vivid emotions and he is ready to depart in peace.

An old man floats about in the sea of his memories like an amoeba in a drop of water, apparently aimless and uncertain. The excitement felt by a man who can concentrate and live over his past is unknown to him. An old man as a rule does not live over the past, he simply reviews it like an outsider watching a drama. He has not learned to expel the accretions and encrustations of old age that prevent any intense reaction or efficient use of his energy. But the good forgetter and the intense living man is often tragic in his memories, when he allows them to come surging into his consciousness. He lives again in the events gone, thrilling with passion, anger or joy, concentrating so intensely on his lost experience that his nerves know the same shiver and shock that the event induced at the time of its happening. His is no calm contemplation that watches the panorama of receding activities. On the contrary, he forces the sun to stand still upon the Gibeon of self while he revels in a resurrected past that is held in the present by the power of his concentration, until through the law of reaction he drops it once more into the abyss of oblivion. By centering his mind on some other object, he forgets it in toto.

4. The Seat of Memory and Imagination in the Physical Body.

The attempt to locate the seat of memory or imagination in the physical body would lead us into inextricable difficulties were we to depart an instant from the hypothesis that has guided us throughout the pages of this book. It is only as we consider that mind and matter are opposite aspects of one process, or as poles of the same thing, that we can connect the two in a logical completeness. If at any time we could find one without the other, we should immediately be thrown into a dualism impossible of solution. By this we do not mean that mind and matter do not appear in a dual aspect. To deny dualism in this sense would be to contradict all the facts. The hypothesis and solution which we hold is a recognition of the greater fact, that through polarity the one substance is expanded into its two aspects, each of equal validity. They support and explain each other. They are opposite aspects of the same process. They are poles of the same thing.

In physical phenomena, by our hypothesis, there can be no memory, only inertia, recurrent action, physical habit, periodic return, repetition of form and persistence of type. Action and reaction being equal, a pure cause injected into a simple environment would produce results which would repeat themselves forever. According to invincible logic, and facts as far as we know them, the universe is an environment containing in itself all causes. It is self-existent and evolves and involves under laws that condition the activity of both matter and mind. It contains the principle of Form and also the principle of Change. The laws which govern in a world of "Forms which change," agreeable to the facts with which they deal, may be stated in reverse terms, applying in this way to both matter and mind. As a result it follows that Form is one aspect or pole of the process or thing, and Change is the other. This being the case, we have laid a foundation for understanding both the physical and mental aspects of memory. Let us illustrate the matter with some of the concepts of geometry.

If one stands directly in front of a circle, it appears before him in perfect roundness. Revolve this circle on its horizontal diameter, and to the sense of sight it changes into a series of ellipses. Of these ellipses each succeeding one shows a diminished minor axis, until the last ellipse merges into a straight line. The observer is the element of rest and the rotating circle is the element of change or motion. Reverse these conditions so that the circle remains stationary and the eye of the observer passes around the circle, and the optical result is the same. First the circle becomes an ellipse; then the ellipse becomes a straight line. Then the straight line expands into an ellipse, and the ellipse becomes the original circle. By a similar relativity of position and motion, a square can be made to appear as a parallelogram, and then to vanish into a line. Lines may be expanded into parallelograms and squares. Right angles can be made to appear as acute angles and acute angles to transform themselves into apparent right angles.

Take any extended object standing before the eye and having appreciable size. Remove it to a distance, and it grows less and less in size. Bring it nearer and it increases. The observer is again the element of rest and the advancing or receding object the element of motion. Again reverse the conditions, so that the object remains stationary and the observer advances or recedes, and the result is the same. If both the observer and the object move so as to retain the same relative positions, there is no apparent change in form. If either rotates on his axis, the other is forced to accelerate his motion in order to maintain the same relative position or point of view.

During these experiments we assume that the normal form and size of the object with reference to other stationary earthly objects has not varied, but the fact remains that a change in the relation of the object to the observer, or of the observer to the object, has resulted in an apparent change in both the form and size of the object. We conclude that motion in either the object or the observer results in a new position, and that a new position gives a new aspect or form to the perceived object. Change in position results in change in form. Although these experiments have to do with the sense of sight, we are warranted in the conclusion that change is inexplicable, except as we posit an original form.

So far, we define change as **form plus motion.**

This brings us to the questions: How is motion at all possible, and what are the exact effects produced by it at the pole of matter and at the pole of mind? In the foregoing illustrations we have treated only of apparent change in form. Let us now penetrate deeper into the matter and formulate our propositions. We must find some yard-stick with which to measure the size of our objects, some standard by which we can judge of the permanence or mutability of our forms. The following propositions are evident.

1. An object to retain a fixed size or form must maintain a fixed relation between its parts.

2. An object may retain a fixed relation between its parts, that is, they may all bear the same internal arrangement and relation to each other, and yet the object can increase or diminish in size. The object can be fixed as to form, but variable as to size.

3. An object that bears a relation to some outside fixed object cannot vary in either form or size without the change being detected.

4. If the outside object and the first object vary together in a like proportion, the change cannot be detected, except by the assistance of a third invariable object.

5. To detect any change there must be a fixed and invariable standard or object.

6. Objects of the same size, form and internal arrangement, in the mind become identified and coalesce, except as they are held apart by being assigned a different relation to some third object.

7. An object of fixed size or form must be capable of assuming an indefinite number of relations to other objects of fixed size and form.

8. All variations in size and form bring variations in the sides or angles of the triangles which establish the forms.

9. An object may retain a fixed size or form itself, and yet by revolving on a central point within it, assume changing relations with other objects.

10. The new form thus created may be detected by any object that has retained relation with some internal or external fixed form.

11. The changeless form which thus establishes and reflects all motions has a cosmic center through which pass all the dimensions of space and time. It is a unity polarized into all created things. It therefore bears a fixed relation to all objects and forms, or, to put it another way, all objects and forms are a part of this archetypal form.

12. Motion may be defined as the ability of a limited portion of this archetypal form or object to draw near to or to depart from another portion of this archetypal form or object. In the physical world this would appear as motion, and in the mental world as imagery or consciousness of form. Even if the archetypal form is changeless, consciousness, by limiting itself to portions of it, will produce varying images and forms. Change likewise will result from the removing limitations from consciousness.

13. Every portion of this archetypal form reflects every other portion. That is to say, each unit of force radicated

in this original form is a part of the whole form and must forever realize and envisage it from its special aspect.

In the foregoing we have tried not to depart from geometrical conceptions concerning which there can be little dispute. Let us now turn to the application of these principles to the problem of memory. Falling back on our hypothesis, we conclude that the Units of Force, which appear in one aspect as matter and in the other as minds, are the constituent parts of the archetypal Form of Existence we have referred to. The Form is the normal relation each bears to the other. It is symbolized by the pure concepts of number and geometry. We further conclude that the relation between the whole and its parts is dynamic.

It is force which expands and sustains the original form, and which brings about all changes and apparent changes within the form.

By our hypothesis, we also conclude that the changes produced by energy will appear at the mental pole as consciousness and in the physical world as motion. Heat expands. Cold contracts. Energy in all forms produces motion. In the mental world, energy is directed by desire. In the physical world, it follows the line of least resistance. From this it follows that the Unit of Force may employ energy at its command to produce change in the physical world, or, in consciousnes, to envisage, expand or contract any portion of this archetypal form. The measure of motion will be that portion of the Form with which the Unit identifies itself. The imagery seen will be the **aspect** of the Form from the particular standpoint chosen, plus all changes produced by the Unit expanding or contracting its consciousnes. In other words, the imagery of any moment of consciousness consists of intuitions of this archetypal form as polarized and affected by the energy of the Unit. Motion and consciousness are possible only by reason of the unity that sustains the form and establishes its parts. Consciousness is also "Form plus motion."

In the foregoing analysis we have been seeking a physical basis for memory. We wish to find the possibility of a synthetic consciousness of experience. We desire a record of each event which memory may synthetize at will, a chain of experiences, any link of which may be revived in consciousness. The record we find is two-faced. It is a polarized process or thing, a form realized through motion. If the Unit is treated as the element of motion, memory consists in the going back to the parts of a fixed record of form. If the Unit is fixed, then the mutations themselves are the record and may unroll themselves in the consciousness of the Unit. In either case, memory deals with a polarized product. Half of it is motion, the other half rest. The unbroken series of changes in experience are as true a record as the seemingly fixed forms of any moment of experience. Memory, grounded in unity and dealing with plurality, sustains the whole. By means of the unity any portion of experience sufficiently energized, or exhibiting sufficient tension, may be brought into consciousness as memory. Forgetting is the disappearance from consciousness of experiences or forms not sufficiently energized.

What is called repetition or recurrent action in the physical world, in consciousness will be the act of remembering. A pendulum swings back again and again to the point of origin of its motion. There are nodal points and oft repeated forms in all rhythmic motion. In mind, these recurrent positions, if brought within the field of consciousness, are memories. They remain memories only so long as they exhibit limited and special aspects of things. Memory is the mental pole of a recurrent process. It recognizes the recurrent positions assumed by the parts of a thing or things because it is the energy of the Unit which makes them assume that position. The intuition of the pure, original form is not memory. A limited and special aspect of the archetypal form is possible by reason of the energy of the Unit. The Unit holds in consciousness only those aspects of the original form it desires. It is concerned only with those changes in which it participates.

From the foregoing, it might appear that we cannot remember, except as we again sense the remembered object in the external world, that the event must return to us, or we go back to it, in either case, to come in contact with the old situation preserved in a material form. True to our law of polarity, we say it makes no difference whether the mind reverts to the remembered position or whether the thing or event appears in consciousness as a present experience. The important point is that these recurrent positions, if accompanied by sufficient tension to bring them into consciousness, appear to the mind as memories. This does not mean that all nature has to repeat herself in order that the mind may reach the recreated form and image it as memory. This, of course, is impossible in the ordinary sense. No past event seems possible of exact duplication in the present. Under our hypothesis, energy proceeds from and pertains to the Unit of Force. It is his energy and none other. It can never be neutralized or brought to quiescence without being returned to him as its source. In like manner, the Unit meeting force with force, is in this unified aspect a pure and simple environment in which all causes repeat themselves and work out their destiny as affected and controlled by the energy of the Unit. In this domain we find the conditions which make recurrent position or memory possible. We also find that unity which permits memory to condense and select those portions of its experiences which are desired in consciousness. If no selection is made, nevertheless the exact memories come themselves. Memory cannot cease until all causes are neutralized and compensated. Even then there will remain the cause of all causes, the possibility of all experiences.

Applying the foregoing to the physical body, we conclude that all sensation arises from motion in the particles of matter of which the body is composed. Physical memory must be a restoration as near as may be of the original conditions in the body at the time of receiving the sensations. With the sense of sight or touch it is not necessary that the nerves carry to the brain and there record the counterpart of the image as sensed. Whatever course the tortuous nerve currents pursue when responding to sense stimuli, we know that consciousness has experienced the sensation in a particular way. For this sensation to reappear as physical memory, somewhere in matter dominated by the field of force of the Unit must reappear the motions which originally presented to consciousness the sensation. The field of force of the Unit, however, in all probability dominates subtler matter and more complex substances than science now connects with the physical body. This cannot receive full explanation until the part played in sensation and memory by these subtler elements is understood. The depth to which consciousnes may penetrate in search for a record or the distance it may travel for an event is limited only by the extent of nature's domain and the profundity of nature itself.

Memory and imagination from the point of view heretofore considered show aspects of both permanence and change. The remembering or imagining subject may be considered as either the element of motion or the element of rest. It is the same with the remembered object or thing. From this we clearly see that the process of memory is dual in its aspect. The contrary principles support each other. Motion is an energized aspect of form. Form is a dynamic relation supported by motion. All experiences are specialized, limited and insulated portions of the one archetypal principle of form, and of the one principle of change or motion. It would be interesting to observe at the mental pole the principles that correspond to insulation of energy and reflection and refraction of rays of light in the physical world. At this place we can only suggest that these principles show the possibility of acquiring a multiplied and varied knowledge of the aspects of an object at one and the same time. Indeed there is possible a completeness of vision which leads to the conception that everything can be seen and envisaged in multitudinous reflections if energy is at hand to break through the ordinary limitations of consciousness. Each Unit is an aspect of and reflects the whole. Breaking through the insulation that masks the particular Units, or by energy enlarging the field of force dominated by the Unit, consciousness may expand without limit, or, as the old books quaintly say, one acquires the power of making himself large or small at will.

5. Abnormal Aspects of Memory and Imagination.

The abnormal aspects which may be assumed by memory or imagination are many. One may stand above or below the average in memory or imagination. In either case, if the difference is pronounced, it will appear abnormal. The secret of good physical memory is good health. Any disturbance that uses energy and withdraws from the brain and nerves a normal and healthful blood supply will interfere with the functions of physical memory. Pain and discomfort in any portion of the body tend to becloud the clear images necessary to good memory and to render difficult and small their associative recall. On the other hand, exhilaration and excitement may brighten the memory and quicken the imagination, to be followed by the reaction of dullness and sluggishness.

The abnormal element in memory and imagination is always some form of unbalance. It arises from too great intensity or too feeble effort. Long continued following out of a single line leads to abnormality. A person may specialize on a given subject until in memory he leaves room for nothing else. He may merely follow an unimportant tendency, as when one becomes continually reminiscent or anecdotal in his habit of thought until everything heard or seen suggests countless incidents, more or less apposite, but tending to crowd out of the mind more valuable growth. The material which fills the mind is usually selected with reference to the ordinary habits and occupation of the person. As more active mental life arises other principles of selection appear. If the tendency in any line is strong, the crop harvested is enormous. Some minds become a jungle of noxious growths selected and nourished by morbid and controlling habits of thought. Even if these accumulations are made casually, but extend over a long period of time, the mass accumulated becomes important and dominates the whole mind.

The energy required to expel from the mind imagery which is not desired is as great as that required to draw in the desirable. In the healthy mind not only must control be had over the expulsion and recall of particular images, but a process of generalization and combination of valuable material must constantly be going on. Without this effort there would be no escape from a mere series of remembered events. This generalizing also consumes energy, but the result is a mental product as available and valuable as the particular images. One would be useless without the other. A completely specialized mind is a mirror that reflects, but never holds or comprehends. The number of memories which may be on call in the forefront of the mind is of necessity limited and depends largely upon the degree of specialization and vitalization of the imagery. One may have at hand a mass of facts no part of which is realized to an extent sufficient to make it forceful or valuable. Little energy is consumed in holding them. The merely encyclopedic mind is seldom great in other respects. On the other hand an idea may be energized and held in mind with a constancy and absorption that excludes all others. It may appear as the passion of genius or the delusion of insanity. Rarely we find a mind tremendous in both specialization and generalization, preserving balance between the two inevitable tendencies, and sitting as a master to guide the interior life of the world.

CHAPTER VIII.

Intuition and Understanding.

1. The Special and the General in Knowledge.

To intuit is to look upon. This is the first and universal meaning of intuition. Translate it into a higher sounding phrase, and you may say intuition is an immediate perception, not a mediate. About an intuition there is no debating. It being a perception the proof is intact. We debate doubtful or undecided subjects. As an intuition is neither doubtful nor undecided, we cannot argue it. But if by its very nature we are debarred from debating about an object of perception, for the looker-on cannot deny that which he sees, nevertheless we may thrash out the problem as to how he came by this absolutely clear and accurate vision.

Knowledge begins with simple sensation, or the direct intuition of object by subject. Consciousness, being the child of object and subject, at one pole exhibits complete objectivity, and at the other abstractions so pure that they seem without content. Lying between these extremes is the great body of knowledge composed of concepts. By our hypothesis all thought is the mental pole of something existing in physical nature. From this it follows that matter must have an aspect corresponding to all mental conceptions of it. It is not a fixed or dead form beheld by intuition. It is not merely the phenomena which reaches us through sensation. Every perceptual change, every conceptual modification in the mind, must have its counterpart and reverse aspect in matter. Knowledge, like consciousness, is a polarized product and comprehended only by realizing the opposing elements of which it is composed. The receptivity of the mind to sensations and the spontaneously arising concepts regarding objects are both a part of conscious life. They rest upon the foundation of an objective material world. They have no existence except as its reverse aspect. Their subtlety is its subtlety. Every possible modification of a concept in thought betokens a change in some realm of physical nature. Sensations of objects are true representations as far as they go, and they and all thoughts about objects cannot in the slightest be divorced from the physical reality of which they are the other pole. Knowledge, therefore, is the mental counterpart of being. To know fully a material thing would be to hold in consciousness the mental pole of all that physically constitutes the object. No object, however, stands entirely alone. It is related to all other objects. It has within it innumerable tendencies and forces. Its aspects are without number. It is the effect of causes that have made it what it is and have assigned to it a particular place in space and time. This being the case, the mere sensing of phenomena gives no knowledge. A mirror reflects, but does not understand. Understanding begins when variety is modified by unity, when the mind recognizes the causes and relations that unite in the perceived form.

One extreme of conscious experience is specialization, and the other pole of the process of thought is generalization. By specialization, we mean an individualized and differentiated experience. In matter, it is merely an evolved and expanded structure or form. It is the climax of effort in a particular direction. The form which results is from resident forces acting through an organism within a particular environment. The consciousness which arises is from energy limited to a determinate compass and directed with the intention of producing a particular result. All specialization uses energy subject to variations in mass and pressure. If the energy available is not large, the tension may be increased by limiting the field of its application. Great results may also be achieved by energy applied towards a special purpose over a long period of time.

Generalization is the exact opposite of specialization.

It is not a diffusion or loss of energy, nor a weakening of the tension and concentration that has resulted in specialization. It is force applied to hold together. It binds and unifies that which is otherwise forced apart. It is the opposite of the active and separating principles that lead to individual experiences and differentiated forms. Intense specialization necessitates somewhere an equally potent generalization.

From the foregoing it will be seen that specialization and generalization must balance each other. To create consciousness or sustain any living form there must be this struggle between the opposites. The binding together and the holding apart are the crossed-beams that support the world. There is no created thing but has this interior structure, no life but is ensouled by this dual force. At the mental pole specialization appears as sensation and the concrete content of experience. Through generalization, however, relations are established and there is understanding.

2. Intuition as an Empirical Judgment or as Pure Knowledge.

We will now depart from the use of the word intuition as meaning a direct sensing of object by subject and speak of it as containing some element of understanding or at least as arriving at results and decisions by processes of the mind too rapid for detection. With reference to intuition in this sense we have two opposing theories. If through intuition we sense objects and reality directly, the question arises as to how much may be included in this contact and how deep the vision may penetrate. Ordinarily we gaze upon a limited field and perceive of objects only their phenomenal aspects. Can intuition become more inclusive? Can it give any true knowledge? If it supplies material to be worked over into knowledge, by what faculty is this done and of what value is the result? Put another way, the question is this:

Is intuition in regard to all things, save perhaps space

and time, a product of evolution plus memory, or is it a faculty of the mind by which given things are seen and known with absolute certainty irrespective of memory (either racial or personal) and properly judged and related? It is said that Herbert Spencer first rationalized the evolutionary hypothesis, explaining by evolution and experience the reason for intuition being in man under one guise, and in the animal and bird under another. We speak of the instinct of the brute and the intuition of man. According to evolution, it would seem that instinct and intuition are but shifting names for one faculty, namely: Memory of the results of past experiences, the experiences themselves forgot. To make the point clearer, we might say intuition in this larger sense and instinct are terms for a memory purged of detail and reduced to its essence, which is tested always by recurring sensations and instinctive reactions rather than by remembered groups of objects. Suppose a man intuitive along a certain line, and no matter whether it refers to locality or personality, he remembers no detailed experiences, but has instinctive feelings and reaction with reference to it. Now, may not these sensations and feelings be the subtle residuum from past experiences, either racial or personal, that, excited by the suggestion of a former environment, appear to him as instincts or intuitions? In other words he revives the emotional reactions of the past, but forgets the details.

The foregoing may properly be styled the evolutionary hypothesis regarding intuition, but there is another hypothesis founded on the Law of Opposites. The doctrine of the Law of Opposites is, that there is nothing in existence, nor conceivable, but is supported by and manifested through opposing principles. All metaphysical and scientific concepts when examined are found to be of this nature. All laws are statable only in contrary terms. By this latter hypothesis, the past in all its fullness supports the present as surely as the present grows out of and balances the past. In the same way the future depends on the present as far as causes are already in operation. Put more accurately, the present is a fulcrum on which balances the past and future. If man has a limited and relative side he must also have an unlimited and absolute side. All causes unite to make him what he is. All existing things bear towards him a determinate relation. According to his polarity or attitude towards his inner or outer universe he will know something or everything about that with which he deals. In agreement with this hypothesis of polarity, if man has the attribute of specializing he must also have the attribute of generalizing; the one being impossible without the other; and by this latter power of generalization he may know infallibly of objects, persons and localities, as surely as he can know partially by his power of specializing. According to this view, instinct in a bird or beast might result from its inclination toward the general rather than the special. Having few experiences, and those along simple lines, and lacking the inordinate self-consciousness of man, it would fall into the universal law of things without resistance, and therefore react accurately. Many other hypotheses have doubtless been advanced in regard to intuition, but these two seem the most worthy of attention.

In studying the problem of intuition we must not overlook the question of energy and its bearing on our power to look on the world and know without apparent effort. We say apparent effort, for there is effort even in looking on, whether the evolutionary or polarity hypothesis be the explanation of it. Not only is the act of intuitive perception an expenditure of energy, but the attaining to the power of such perception through experience, whether personal or racial, has been through an enormous expenditure of energy. No matter where or how stored it cannot violate the fundamental law of cause and effect. Action and reaction must be equal. Nor can the polarity hypothesis be imagined an escape from a serious expenditure of energy. For the mind to generalize to the point of absolute certainty, resulting in instantaneous perception, is to open the valve of the engine called man, and let all the steam escape at once. Consciously or unconsciously, a man with all knowing power along one line has dissipated himself over the whole expanse of the subject by one supreme effort, and well nigh loses his hold on individuality in the attempt. For the same reason the greatest specialist along any line is consciously or unconsciously the greatest generalist in connection with it, and has therefore the largest amount of intuition in regard to it. Again arises the question of energy. As the Unit of Force is limited in its power to generate energy, no man can generalize over more than a limited expanse of the universe at any one time without losing individuality and abandoning individual purposes. So, to be a specialist in any subject, is to be equal to a complete generalization of it almost to the exclusion of all other subjects. We would call such a person a great specialist, but very narrow as to general knowledge outside of his specialty, and this would be true because of his limit in energy. As to his specialty, however, he would be a generalist with a superb intuition.

Let us illustrate this point by reference to the instincts of animals. Suppose a homing pigeon to have a restricted range of ideas as to the universe at large, specializing on locality only, so that his love of home is balanced with the power of absolute universality in regard to it. The very limitation of this pigeon's idea-conceiving power enables him through his unit of energy (itself being constant) to perfect himself along the line of his specialization even to the generalizing of it into accurate instinct. So also with the bee, the beaver, in fact all the lower grades of animal and insect life. Energy, then, is at its limit in an individual's power to generalize. Even time itself, according to the Kantian conception, is an a priori pure intuition of the mind. Specializations in time result because man finds himself lacking in power to generalize upon the formal whole of time at once. Having insufficient force to stay the stream, he must generalize and specialize successively so as to focus here and there until like a spider he spins his web of specialization and generalization about himself consistently with his point of view and the strength of his Unit of Force.

According to this analysis the specialist is ordinarily narrow, but a great generalist within his limit, and possesses intuition either through memory of his experiences, racial or personal, or because of polarity, and the power temporarily to shift the poles of his being. If this be true, the individual whose Unit of Force is great, having in himself a constant but enormous capacity for the generation of energy, will have a wider range in which to universalize a subject or himself. He will appear to the world to be less of a specialist than he really is. He gets out of sight of human judgment because he reaches so far. Like the great thinker he is, if he chooses to draw himself in and come down upon any special subject, he handles it with weight. Such an individual has a marvelous intuition about many things rather than few. He speaks with authority. He is an oracle; and his judgment is usually final and unanswerable. However great he may be, he still uses his powers subject to the law of conservation of energy. In dealing with matters which he has not comprehended either through generalization or specialization he will show ordinary fallibility. His great powers subject him to special temptations and misunderstandings. Intuitive and true in many things and conscious of his ability to fathom almost any matter by a few moments of concentrated effort, if he foregoes this necessary expenditure of energy, he will encounter the errors and mistakes common to all.

3. Growth and Change in Knowledge.

If one understands a thing, he not only perceives it and can act with reference to it, but can reason about it. Understanding implies subtlety and depth. To understand any object is to get a thorough grasp on it with the tentacles of the mind. You sense it, you relate it, you weigh, measure and qualify it. Specially, you grapple with its individuality; generally, you relegate it to a class of its own. "With all thy getting, get understanding." That is, know the matter in hand as thoroughly as the human mind finds possible. Know your limitations as well as your capabilities. Know what you can and what you cannot know. Realize negatively all that you do not comprehend positively. Without this knowledge of the mind's capabilities and limitations your understanding is at fault. Without knowledge of the limitations imposed, it is not understanding at all, but misconception and error, those ghosts of the dark which lead men into pitfalls out of which they find it hard to climb. The majority of mankind understand from one pole or the other of their being with faulty perception and reason. Not being directly under the proposition or thing they are investigating, they get a side-glance view and consequently lose balance in judgment. This method leads to fatal shams and delusions with which the world seems teeming. Man fails to meet objectivity fairly and squarely with subjectivity. He looks at the universe from the corners of his eyes, or with a pronounced squint, and presumes to claim as his prerogative an understanding of that which he refuses to meet with a full glance. Hence our cranks, our pseudo-philosophers, our false prophets, our frauds. The tree of life and knowledge has roots as well as branches and leaves. If its root-nature, more especially its tap-root nature, is studied, its growth and bloom can be quite readily comprehended. But who, save a real thinker or one gifted with marvelous intuition, ever thinks of burrowing like a mole at the root of things? Your pseudo-philosopher makes a hammock of the boughs of this mystical tree and swings back and forth among its green leaves and flowers, warbling his opera-bouffe of apparent profundities to a vast audience that gathers from far to drink in his gushing words. A true thinker may get hold of a thing and understand it with lightning quickness, or he may plod for it. Whichever his way, he has squeezed it like a lemon dry of its juice and quaffed the elixir to the last drop. A man may have an a priori grasp on something he desires to know or he may logically analyze and synthesize it till its parts, united or separated, are within his ken. He may also realize what he cannot know in regard to it; then, as far as human terms and capacity go, he may be said to have understanding of it.

Mind, pure and simple, is built from a logical base. By necessity its only method of true and honest expression is the logical method. Logos is intrinsic in mentality as well as in morality. It is Logos; and when the oracular word is voiced through intellect or heart we say, "It is spoken." The "logic of events" we might call causality; a pure logic, necessity. While the mind is beaded in logic—with concepts and judgments set in it like jewels in a ring—in one sense we no more comprehend it than do we the Newtonian law of gravitation. When clearly seen, the fact is treated as an intuition, seems self-evidenced and is no longer debatable. As it is impossible to conceive of two and two making other than four, so it is impossible to escape logic in the texture of the mind or in the operation of its laws when once grasped.

At this point in our reasoning we are estopped and dumb. Thus far and no farther can we understand. The interaction of law and laws is quite easily in our grasp, but the Law! Can the included ever grasp that which includes it? Can a part envelope the whole? Or may it be that in reverse aspect the part cannot be less than the whole? This is true logical polarity and the only solution of this antinomy of reason that forever confronts us. The opposite of quantity is quality, and reason is only true to itself in insisting that in quality it is the whole and that by reflection the whole appears in each part. It is by limitation that specialized experiences are gained, and their very intensity and distinct objectivity betoken the concentrated energy which shuts out the larger view.

Times and spaces are but limitations of one Time and one Space, either of which conceived or grasped in its pure form reverses its aspect and seems a different product. Causality reduces itself to rhythms of action and reaction. All things are the polarized product of a self-generating, self-existent universe and mind. Unified and self-existent only in its completeness and sufficiency, for by its inextinguishable polarity it gets back all its parts, creates and supports all things and lives its objectified thoughts and experiences forever. By our hypothesis, the laws of mind are but the laws of external nature in reverse aspect, and they will operate to strew the world with the intellectual corpses of those who fail to understand them or to adjust the mental half of their being to their sway.

Looking at nature externally, we see only matter and its motions. In such a world a body never lacks reality. By its very nature it is substance and objectified. Although shaped by internal forces and governed by invisible laws, the constancy of these laws supplies us with all we know about external nature. The imagery of sensation is not knowledge, and the phenomenal aspects of things ordinarily presented to us, however attractive for the moment, would lose meaning and interest if we did not begin to analyze out and understand the law back of the phenomenon. It is finding the norm, the constant, the law, that gives us knowledge. All classifying of phenomena under concepts is a part of this irresistible tendency. All laws by their very nature are changeless and perfect, and like regular geometrical figures are but parts of a more inclusive perfect Form and Law.

The one law that is constant through all variety is that, given forces once in operation, the mathematics of combination and change must prevail. This creation of differentiated and specialized forms is inevitable and the very gist of the law. If force is generated or manifested at all it must act according to its quantity. Mass is but the quantity of resistence, or inertia, which meets or carries a given force. When force meets force there is increase of manifestation by combination or decrease by neutralization. From this it will be seen that all motion, generated by forces, must operate according to the law of action and reaction. Motion is by its very nature rhythmical. Viewed statically the resulting phenomena show polarized and opposite aspects.

While the forces in nature are never seen and all conceptions of them are supplied by the mind, they are nevertheless forces. The internal consciousness or comprehension of them is the other half of them. Under our hypothesis they cannot exist in any other way. They form the body of what Kant would call non-sensuous knowledge, and must exist in reverse aspect in some consciousness in order to be forces at all. They are the very laws of nature and operate in her ways.

The question of understanding resolves itself into a question of personality. Is there either within or without a unit of individuality which holds in its grasp all that may enter into consciousness and in that wonderful comprehension establishes all relations and understands? It is evident that the subject which perceives all else as object is such a unit. In understanding, it and the object are one. This being the case, it makes no difference whether a principle or law is first observed or grasped internally or externally. The law discovered will operate in both realms. Force is constant. The rhythms of cause and effect are sure. Knowledge is always self-knowledge and, dealing with forces, is and will be power. The internal world is of the same magnitude and complexity as the external. Of necessity it must exactly balance it. Understanding is knowledge of the laws under which operate the forces that unite the two realms.

From the foregoing it will be seen that, with reference to knowledge, there is growth and change. From an individual viewpoint, all sensation is partly grounded in chaos and therefore imperfectly interpreted and understood. To understand a given experience, we must analyze its parts and establish all its relations. It must be grasped spatially, temporally, and with reference to causes that unite in it and effects that flow from it. This being the case, it is evident that there are all gradations of understanding of things and events. All laws manifest and operate in each thing, but individuality is fixed by the predominance of some particular law. Ordinarily we seek only the law or principle of which we desire to make use. Man returns again and again to his rejected by-products to extract from them rare elements, glorious essences and colors. For nature herself there is no waste or by-product. All operates according to law. Each event is a perfect sequence of cause and effect.

4. The Body of Knowledge.

"Unwritten laws; eternal in the heavens; not of today or yesterday are these, but live from everlasting and from whence they sprang none knoweth."

What we call a law in external nature is internally an Idea. This is an old and honorable use of the word. It is a suitable name for the reverse aspect of a law, but we seem to have forgotten the dynamic feature which attached to the doctrine as originally taught. With a revival of interest in the study of external nature and a searching out of her laws, there must come a like discernment of the internal aspect of the laws. Without an appropriate substitute for this ancient teaching of Plato, science is hindered and cramped in its effort to interpret the external world. With a clear perception of the nature and relationship of Ideas, all investigation of external nature would be given a new impetus and meaning, balance would be preserved in understanding, and growth in knowledge be secure. Energy once used to comprehend the working of a law brings order out of chaos and incorporates the results in the observer. To the extent the law operates, that particular realm is ever afterwards accessible and more easily controlled.

If knowledge is a comprehension of the laws according

to which operate the forces of nature, then it must have a body to correspond with the organic complexity of those laws. Strictly speaking, a law of nature is neither internal, nor external, but, like all things in a world of polarity, exhibits two aspects. In one aspect it is merely the rule by which the forces of nature, measured according to quantity, operate. It is the mathematics of combination and change. In the other aspect it is a prototype or form which exhibits the result of the working of the law. This being the case, the infinite variety of forms actually realized or conceivable is the only limit that can be placed on the number of laws. Mathematics does not pretend to limit the number of its geometrical shapes nor will algebra cease to elaborate expressions, formulae and series. Reduce the present world to mathematics, and, in the act, the variety of new combinations possible will be so apparent that the inexhaustible nature of experience is at the same time proved. This being the case, we see that Idea, or Form, is internally the free and creative aspect of what externally is matter moving according to determinable laws and with mathematical exactitude. Were it otherwise, there could be neither certainty nor knowledge. The past would lie unexplained and the future remain unrevealed. Mathematics is the opposite of free will, the other half of it. With causes once in operation, the mathematics of combination and change must prevail.

For Form to exist at all it must have expression in matter. Originally Form is pure as distinguished from applied mathematics. By reason of it, synthetic judgments a priori are possible, or in other words pure Form is a solvent of both the static and dynamic features of any event. This being the case, the body of knowledge referred to in this paragraph is a Kingdom of Forms or visible expressions of invisible laws. In becoming visible all forms are dependent on matter, or strictly put, appear as matter.

By our hypothesis, there is no consciousness that is not grounded in an objective, material pole. The body of knowledge, therefore, is the order appearing in external nature by reason of its dependence on law and form. The extent to which this is realized in consciousness depends upon the individual, but whether comprehended or realized, it is still a kingdom which he maintains and by which he is controlled.

5. Abnormal Aspects of Knowledge.

From all we can gather as to the dialectic method of reasoning we surmise that it is a perfectly true and logical method and only destructive when universalized through misjudgment in its manipulation. A yard stick measures a yard and is true to itself, but if some egoist gets hold of it and asserts that it measures a mile he is "Beyond dispute."

The dialectic method was the Platonic and is now used altogether by modern schools of thought. It is simply an inductive logic, nothing more nor less, and therefore used by science along special lines. In fact it is the reasoning of specialism rather than generalism. A dialectic reasoner gets hold of a datum and runs it to the ground. His curiosity is almost absurd. He pries, he spies and impudently asks questions like Socrates till his gourmand intellect is satiated along some particular line. Now, if he is wise in his dialectic or inductive method he will not attempt the drawing out of the universe through one needle's eye. On the contrary, he will know his values and assets and for just how much they count. In dialectically evolving a fish's eye, he establishes its history by an analysis and induction of the facts involved, but he does not necessarily find a beginning for the world or a divine authority for hell. His logic is true enough in its inductive method, but he, himself, if he so departs, is not true to it. The Kantian dialect, therefore, resolves itself into chaos only from an attempt to make it produce the results of transcendental logic. Logic in a sense is polarized into the deductive and inductive. From the perfection of deduction or from wholeness or law we strike out at specials and by the subtle penetration of induction we approach unity.

The mistake man makes in handling this two-edged sword of logic is that of striving for the fruits of induction through the deductive method and for the fruits of deduction through the inductive method. The reason why Kant calls dialectic destructive is simply because of the abuse of it in the common mind.

In the finality of reasoning either all is illusion as far as man's understanding of things goes or there is no illusion. Man looks out upon objectivity and his face to a good physiognomist tells how he views it and what he sees. Some behold specials in excess of generalities and vice-versa. Again a rare soul gets an approximately balanced view, seeing wholes and parts, and these same parts properly related. Now illusion, in the ordinary understanding of the term, would seem to be the disease of the vast majority in whom specialization over-balances generalization, the parts of their whole being misfilled or improperly related to one another. An individual who looks on objectivity after this manner fails to co-ordinate things. Causes and effects becoming divorced, he finds himself in a maze of illusion, which is all the more misleading because he fails to recognize it as such. His obstinacy is superb. He sees a thing so and so and therefore it is so and so. Now we do not believe in discrediting the senses. We touch the world with them, get our images of outsideness through them. Nevertheless, a deluded individual practically stops there, while a balanced person brings comparison, co-ordination and understanding to bear on the impressions captured through the eyes, ears and touch. He not only senses, he relates, reasons, decides. In other words, he deals logically with all images photographed on his sensitive subjectivity.

A child beholds the moon on the rim of the East as large as a barrel hoop. The sage sees the same phenomenon. To both it is apparently the same size. There is no mistake about the law of imagery from light rays, but the child stops there and lives in illusion. The scientific man, however, takes account of distance, locality, the eye, light and its principles, the reflecting power of the moon, etc., etc., and decides that while he saw correctly, nevertheless the little planet is equal in size to a habitable globe. In this way a wise man can distinguish illusion from fact and in specializations safely trust his senses as guides.

But how about generalization and the hidden dynamics which act under the guise of law? Here most certainly the would-be sage is likely to fall victim to illusion, mistaking hypothetical matters for facts and dealing with theories as though they were proved. This attitude toward the abstract flounders him in a quagmire and makes him utterly incapable of heading any line of scientific research. One must approach a possible principle very cautionsly, as though it were dangerous. He must touch this live wire of a law with gloved hands, for he does not know it, why it is or what it is, and he should be exceedingly humble. Right here let us refer to the much used term, "self-evident." Why do two and two make four? "Because it couldn't make anything else. We know it from self-evidence." But what is self-evidence? This kind of reasoning results in the Ego's clawing itself with its own talons. In other words, it is useless and proves at once that the unknowable is unknowable. If this be so, it reveals an abyss into which an incautious thinker is liable to fall. Probably his hypothesis is not a law at all but an illusion. In that case he would better steer clear of it. If, however, he has in grasp an eternal principle, newly discovered, he should remember it is dynamic and in its essence undiscoverable. This attitude assumed toward the abstract will most likely protect him from illusion. His limitations standing fixed he will recognize them and find protection in them. The law of cause and effect in specialization being apparent, he will grapple with things, and, understanding their relationship, become a master of life and its possibilities. But he is exceptional.

Humanity en masse is peculiarly polarized. In feeling it exercises common sense, but in thinking is easily duped. The balance, however, is approximately struck or the word "peace" would be unknown in its vocabulary. But let an individual emerge from the mob and cudgle his brains and try to think and regulate his feelings accordingly, leaving so-called instinct to bees and birds and substituting a new-born reason in its place. Then let the world look out. The chances are nine out of ten that this immature thinker will either be swamped in the sea of his own delusions or become by his absurdity the laughing stock of his age. But the tenth mortal like the tenth muse will probably receive the gift of immortality and live through the ages.

We have thus far been dealing with the subject of illusion and error as an unbalance between specialization and generalization resulting in a failure to understand. There is also fraud, lying, deception and related abnormalities based on deliberate perversion of truth rather than on mistake. A full treatment of these topics must be left to Ethics, but we can here point out how actual fraud and deception is but an effort to prolong the illusion, under which the person is suffering. Illusion means nothing except as it brings to a person the conviction or belief that something exists in a particular way. The observer is not under the illusion unless he believes it does exist. Inasmuch as all things are possibilities and exist in potentiality, the illusory something, if imaginable, cannot be denied a certain reality. The mistake is to assign it erroneously to a particular time and place or to attempt to bring it within a particular rhythm of cause and effect. Now the intellect may shake itself free from the error before the desires are done with trying to reap the fruits of the imagined or illusory situation. In such a case lying and deception may be resorted to in order to bring others under the illusion or maintain them in their error. Few are strong enough to realize the price they will ultimately pay in energy, with attendant emotions, before they bring order out of this chaos willfully brought into their lives.

Man is easily the dupe of any sharp designer, and deluded as to the person with whom he deals. This same evil person may give truth; for the Devil can appear as an angel of light. Many cults have been forced on humanity by self-seeking fakirs, and yet the cults have lived and been to an extent a benefit to the world. All this shows that truth cannot be entirely disguised even by the veil of illusion. In the finality of reasoning, either all is illusion as far as man's understanding goes, or there is no illusion. If man is not prepared by cause and effect in specials, all specials will play him false. If he is irreverent towards generals, the law will turn and rend him. But if he knows that he does not know and what he does know, he is never deluded, for, by realizing the illusion, to him as illusion it ceases to be.

CHAPTER IX.

Periodicity.

1. Motion and Rest.

In treating of motion and rest we will consider them compound rather than simple. Like all important concepts each is an element in a pair. The single concept is meaningless except as understood in connection with its companion. Although the terms are antithetical, the paradox is only seemingly untrue. Each concept is supported by its opposite, the parallelism being complete. The contrary aspects are views of the opposite poles of the same thing.

This being the case, we conclude that the thing or event for which the concept stands is polarized. By polarity we mean separated into parts, while still retaining a unity that makes one thing. Events or phenomena we define as the experience of things. Externally this experience is motion. Internally it is consciousness or recognition of change. We are here at the fundamental point in our philosophy and must further explain and justify the hypothesis of this book. Under our hypothesis, there can be no phenomena without polarization and no polarization without Units of Force. Mind and matter, being opposite poles of the same thing, in this sense constitute only a simple. But the unity thus conceived of is polarized. Given two, necessitates innumerables. Each part is in quality the whole and exhibits polarity. At the mental pole there is unity. In matter there is always variety and parts.

When we declare that motion and rest are opposite poles of the same thing we mean it in both the conceptual and in the literal and actual sense. One may become the other at any time. At the poles each reverses itself and becomes the other. Motion infinitely rapid or infinitely slow merges into rest. Rest, or matter at rest, is inconceivable except as made up of parts in periodic motion.

At one pole the mind views rest, at the other pole, motion. At one pole we move through the world and are subject to its forces. At the other pole the world is contained in us and does our bidding. But the consciousness of the Unit may at any time shift to the opposite pole. As in trigonometry, an element which passes through unity or infinity changes its algebraic sign.

By this same law, we see that the opposite poles or characteristics of any event or thing are linked in indissoluble union. The mind or ego commands each, but in viewing one merges itself in the other. Consciousness arises from this polarity, whether or not it be analyzed or understood. So complete in application is the law, that we say it cannot be stated or grasped, except as the Unit of Force polarizes itself in a higher degree and stands back of both rest and motion as an unmanifested and unexpressed third, which is neither motion nor rest, but supports the two. This recession stands as a self-established series, infinite, simple, sure.

By the law of opposites, all the parts and derivatives of any process or thing are permanent, though special, aspects of the thing. The compression and dynamic force of this concept is so great that it will penetrate and account for all that is. If no element of change or instability is detected in it, it is a law in which the mind will find peace; a rock by which physical things are supported and upon which we stand. It is the changeless law that accounts for change. Motion and rest are here forever combined. They support and explain each other. They are fundamental aspects of Units of Force. They are opposite poles of the same thing.

2. Force and Consciousness.

We have shown in the preceding paragraph how the Units of Force of our hypothesis combine in themselves both rest and motion and are therefore true entities. On account of this polarity they are able to participate in every event and to account for all phenomena. In them motion is grounded in rest and change supported by permanence. This being the case, they are immortal. By the very law of their being, sequence in all their experiences, or cause and effect united, is absolute. The presence in consciousness of the whole rhythm of any given experience is immaterial, for the known is fruit of the unknown, just as the unknown is inherent in the known. Each supports and explains the other. They are opposite poles of the same thing.

Force is evidently dynamic, supplementing matter, and though apparently inseparable from substance, we nevertheless define it as Cause, and Energy as that same fundamental cause expressed. Force is never realized in consciousness, for as soon as it manifests it is energy or an output. Force is unknowable, but energy can be reckoned upon, and rhythm is the key of it. Force per se is beyond understanding, but it would seem to be simple and a generator of perpetual motion. That which appears in consciousness is called energy, and is immersed in objectivity, expressing in duality as one and many.

We assert that we cannot know the mystery of force by itself, and yet we give it seeming attributes; but these same apparent attributes are only surmised through our knowledge of energy, and make still more mysterious the generator behind it. We call it force for need of a better term, as we call matter dust for the same reason.

But energy, on the contrary, ever active in manifestation, is subject to the law of mathematics, and is reckoned by periodicity. Space and time are necessary to it; in fact matter conditions it and makes possible our dealing with it. Periodicity is but the tidal ebb and flow of energy conditioned by matter. Now matter may easily be defined as the stress and strain of energy in its dualistic manifestation or output, this same stress and strain appearing in gas, liquid, hardness, softness, etc. It does not in the least concern us how we define or analyze this "dust," in the question of periodicity. We will call it by its everyday name—matter, and study its rhythmic assumptions through its energetic expressions.

Mathematically speaking, if man were subtle enough he could calculate on the tides of being with absolute exactness, but the intricacy of a wheel within a wheel, or a rhythm within a rhythm, makes a problem of incalculable complexity and almost impossible of solution.

As all dust energized is rhythmic in its activities, and as dust or matter varies in density, etc., its different expressions have varying tides, acting and reacting upon each other, producing infinite varieties in potential and kinetic expressions, sleeping and waking, negatives and positives, that while big with life are nevertheless so sphinx-like in their inter-dealings that an Oedipus or a Laotsze could hardly compass them. Nevertheless the rhythm or periodicity is everywhere discoverable, and the law may be posited in defiance of opposition and proven here and there through experience. It is not hard to get special illustrations of rhythm, but as one mounts upward toward generalization, finding the rhythm of rhythms, or the periodicity of periods, relating and balancing the small and great, though the principle stands a mountain beneath his feet, yet the marshalling of data, and the relativities of the same are almost beyond his intellect; he grows dizzy grappling with this marvelous mathematical complexity based on a single law.

In his own body man finds this dominating principle crying out in continual expression—"thus far and no farther." Man is a tidal being, a creature of ebb and flow, mounting to climaxes and subsiding by reaction to whence he started. Each moment contains its rhythm, each hour, day, week, month, year, life; so slight in an instant of time that he is utterly unconscious about it, but in longer periods becoming exceedingly evident and called by him, most appropriately, his moods.

Now force, conceived of as simple, could have no moods, and only under mathematical stress and strain in coming out as energy can it be subjected to reaction through action. Action and reaction are equal, and there is no true and sustained pause anywhere, only an apparent breathlessness of being as the "tide turns."

Force manifesting as energy appears in two ways, namely, centripetal and centrifugal; but this latter expression of it, namely, the centrifugal, is not the true force, but is due to the law of inertia. For instance, in the whirl and spin of energized matter all its atoms tend toward a common center, but through their very stress and strain to reach the desired heart of things throw off at a tangent a certain proportion; in other words, crowd them out, and they, thrown off and inert, speed directly ahead, going on indefinitely till through friction with whatever they contact they are deflected and perhaps recaught by the attraction of the mass from which they came. So then the one centripetal force, by its very intensity toward centralization, is manifested in its opposite aspect of so-called centrifugal force. But it should be remembered that the tendency is not in the hypothetical atoms to fly off, but in energy to over-centralize itself and consequently to throw them off.

Now all this bears on rhythm, and really explains periodicity. Inertia could never be realized without this very extravagance of energy. Polarity is discoverable in this way, and the negatives and positives are made apparent.

In the stress, strain and whirl of energy in the being called man, he attains to consciousness of rhythm, and realizes his centralizations and his escapes, his homogeneous and heterogeneous tendencies, his evolution toward organism and his dissolution into elements. One condition he knows to be synthetic and the result of a purposeful energy, the other a chaotic state due to inertia and expulsion.

Having become by experience and inference conscious of this law as the base of his existence, he may in time ascertain its working in practical life and in a way be prepared for its tidal expression, and by this very preparation in a manner forestall his moods; that is, admitting the law of periodicity based on the nature of energy in matter, man is at once, in a sense, the king of it rather than the slave. Instead of blindly submitting to his tidal states of being, he transcends without annihilating them. At a climax he prepares for a descent and is never surprised. In the depths he girds up for a climb to the heights, sure of reversal of fortune by the very nature of rhythm itself. If one life does not suffice to prove the principle, another is sure to follow; for the law stands.

We have studied the question of force sufficiently to discover that we know nothing of its ultimate attribute, but about energy or its manifestation we can posit characteristics. Energy we know polarizes into activity and inertia, expressing in periodicity or rhythm. But looking deeper we find another attribute in nature, namely, that of purpose or will. This latter never in the least destroys rhythm, but may most decidedly regulate it, using time and space as factors by which so to do.

For instance, a man may spend six months or six years building a house, the structure being upon the same original plan in either case, but whether he takes six months or six years, the same amount of energy is expended either way; or he may use energy in patterning it into a shape quite different from the original plan, provided an equation is struck.

This erratic attribute in energy that we call will or desire may even exercise itself chaotically, with intention, over-throwing and destroying rather than in synthetic determinateness in building.

Applying this factor in energy to the study of rhythm, we find that man may dwindle or enlarge his periodicities without for an instant destroying them. He may blow up his house with dynamite and prevent its normal decay, he may kill himself with poison and escape the death of age. The same energy is expended either way, he simply controls the time it takes to do it. When man becomes conscious of his power to yoke periodic energy to the steed of Time, he becomes a high ruler among the Gods. He cannot escape rhythm, but he can make it so short or so long that it escapes him in consciousness, and to all intents and purposes, "he takes his life in his own hands."

Normal evolution is the slow, long, rhythmic expression of aeonic tides of energy, but when self-consciousness is fully attained the work of an aeon may be done in a century and that of a century extended through a cycle.

Herein lies the open secret of the game of "hide and go seek," forever being played between will and periodicity. The attributes of energy defy and foil each other, and thus develop in the very essence of being the sense of supreme consciousness.

All force, under our hypothesis, is one in quality. Manifested as energy, forces may unite to produce greater results, or they may neutralize and counteract each other. Energy neutralized, however, is not energy lost. It is simply taken up and absorbed so that it disappears from manifestation. All energy has this solvent quality and is transmutable into other forms. When once manifested, all that distinguishes one force from another is its insulation and its quantity. This being the case, the fundamental question for psychology is to find out how energy is generated and what determines its quantity. By our hypothesis, minds are "Units of Force, each having the power to generate a constant but limited amount of energy, and no two alike in quantity."

Looking at nature externally, we see nothing that shows how energy is generated or that gives individuality to force. There are no units of force which appear permanently such. Material bodies with which we come in contact are only carriers of energy. All masses of matter are aggregates and compounds. It is true, physical bodies seem to carry definite amounts of energy, but it is of their very nature to absorb other energy and to radiate and disperse what they possess. In observing them we find no determinate core of individuality, no spontaneous generator of force. Looking internally, the case is reversed. Consciousness is ever asserting the will and desire to do something. The inner self is a fountain of energy. It generates and gives forth illimitably, but, as we contend, invariably receives back its own. We therefore maintain that each Unit of Force is differentiated from all others by the quantity of its energy. Out of this difference arises all motion. Without it the interdealing of the units could not be maintained.

Inasmuch as sensation is dependent upon motion, and motion is but the manifested aspect of energy, we see that force and consciousness are opposite poles of the same thing. This being the case, they are also exactly opposite in characteristics. What you can posit of one pole you cannot posit of the other. All that appears at one pole will appear in reverse aspects at the other. From this it follows that force is unthinkable and in itself unknown. It is the unknowable pole of what appears as consciousness. Known only in consciousness, there can be no grasp of either force or consciousness, except as we discover the law that conditions both. If force in becoming manifested or known is consciousness, by the same law it is apparent that when we lose consciousness, or swing to the pole of rest, we release energy and make it available as an apparently new force. This rhythm of polarized activity is the key to an understanding of most of our mental processes. In the physical world we trace the energy involved in chemical and physical phenomena, so at the mental pole we may know that each shifting from the conscious to the unconscious pole of being is but following a law that preserves balance in our lives, conditions all our activities, and is at the very foundation of all consciousness whatsoever. Without it there could be no consciousness. By reason of it, consciousness is the mate of unconsciousness and as eternal and sure.

If sensation is dependent upon motion and all motion is but the manifested aspect of force, it follows that where there is motion there is consciousness, and that without motion there is no consciousness. As we have seen, however, all motion is relative. At the nodal points rest becomes motion and motion becomes rest, accordingly as the consciousness of the observer is fixed. The standpoint or polarity of the observer, therefore, with reference to motion and rest becomes crucial. Consciousness is also relative. The unconscious of today is the conscious of tomorrow. Also, by the law of opposites, what is unknown to you is known to some opposing consciousness, the balance being rhythmically maintained and complete. There is no shifting of polarity without passing through unconsciousness. The limitation is imposed by the very nature of polarity.

It is the holding apart and binding together that supports the world.

From the foregoing it follows that all consciousness is no consciousness. The poles meet in perfect poise. Such a state is reached by either inclusion or exclusion. Passing through infinity or unity, each element changes its sign. Force passing through the Unit becomes multiple as quantitative energy. Consciousness passing through unconsciousness restores to the Unit its force and the possibility of new experience.

Memory and experience show us a perfect succession of rhythms of consciousness and unconsciousness, activity and rest in any one medium or grade of matter being quantitatively balanced. One cannot draw in without giving out. He cannot observe phenomena without in the act setting up the rhythm that drags them from him. Finding the law constant, we calculate by it and make it our foundation.

3. Rhythm and Orbital Motion.

True to the law of opposities, polarity itself exhibits both static and dynamic aspects. All space is polarized, there being no such thing as extension without polarity. The simplest expression of the static aspect of polarity is the straight line. To conceive of it, one must as it were mark one end with the "+", the other with the "—" algebraic sign. In order to have the positive or the negative, there must also be the neutral point that separates the two.

The dynamic feature of polarity is rhythm. The simplest expression of this is the swinging pendulum. A pendulum swings through an arc subtended by a chord. It can swing in no other way, yet it arrives in its oscillations at the points established by the termini of the chord. From this we see that motion is inherently rhythmical and yet indissolubly connected with its static pole of a fixed form. What this union is, is a mystery, but it is apparent that motion and rest are opposite poles of one process or thing.

If motion is the dynamic pole of rest and visible form, then it follows that rhythm is the only true expression of motion. By rhythm we mean simply the positive and negative aspects of motion shown in recurrent positions and states. These recurrent positions appear in all motion, action and reaction being equal. Any deviation from motion along the lines of a fixed form arises from a new force affecting the original motion. Where two or more forces act on a moving body the result is rhythmical motion.

The difference between motion and rest appears to be merely one of polarity. Force applied in one direction produces motion, and the same amount of force applied in the opposite direction produces rest. The rest thus produced, however, has taken up the energy manifested by the force. By all our hypotheses, the object retains internally the motion or disperses it as light, heat or some other form of energy. This being the case, it is apparent that a body in motion cannot reach a state of rest without giving off energy or converting it into internal motion. This internal motion in turn gives it all its characteristics as a body and makes it a seemingly extended and static thing. According to the polarity, i. e., position of the plane of wave motion, it will affect other vibrations and appear as a fixed object or thing. Rest, therefore, we define as internal and approximately balanced motion. That which is balanced internally does not actively disturb or affect others, and appears at rest. Motion too rapid or too slow to interfere materially with this internal motion will not set going vibrations sufficient to affect our consciousness or even make the object visible or appear as a thing. Things are systems of motion dominated by some unit of force.

When we say that motion is inherently rhythmical we do not mean that it cannot assume any form. The primal impulse of all force is to act in a straight line. Indeed, it seems always so to act, manifesting as attraction or the tendency to directly contact its object. Thus set in motion it becomes quantitative energy and must remain such until transformed by some polarizing act of the Unit of Force. But force cannot manifest as energy except as it encounters other forces. Matter is dependent upon the strain and stress between units of force. There must be both action and reaction. Without this, energy would not be apparent and would have no carrier. When force is once manifested as energy, its true expression is action and reaction or rhythmic motion. Rhythmic motion, however, is not confined to the simple swing of the pendulum. The real tendency is towards a greater arc of completer form of motion. If sufficiently energized the pendulum will swing in a circle around the central point. The central point in turn is never at rest so the true tendency or form of rhythmic motion is spiral. Spheroidal shapes and cones, traced by spirals of motion, exhibiting in cross-section approximate circles, ellipses, parabolas and hyperbolas, are the curious fruits of the orbital motion which determines the periodic function of the energy of Units of Force.

4. Law and Laws.

Under our hypothesis consciousness results whenever force becomes energy, or in other words, is polarized into motion. Energy in turn is conditioned by matter, space and time being necessary to it. This being the case, we see that motion, in space and time, and conditioned by matter, is necessary to energy, and is the law under which it operates, a necessary condition of its manifestation. In this principle of necessity for specialization, we find the one Law of all manifested life, the Parent Cause of all the special tendencies or laws revealed in its working. Both the Law and the laws are permanent, invariable, constantly working, inevitable. In their nature independent and unconditioned, a law grasped is a slave forever. Given the necessity for specialization of the Law, which is merely the mathematics of combination or environment, the laws, or tendencies resulting from the rhythmic assumptions of energy in the interdealing of the Units of Force, are a limitless field of experience operating with mathematical exactitude, yet based on a single Law. In this book, therefore, we deal only with forces operating according to law.

The necessity for a physical body is a direct result of the operation of this necessity for specialization. Force manifested is energy. Energy is periodic, or reckoned as rhythmic motion. Rhythmic motion results in a system of motion dominated by some Unit of Force. We, therefore, conclude that every Unit of Force is capable of polarizing itself into countless units and of maintaining them as a self-centered constellation or universe of motion. This internal universe is mind or the free and unconditioned aspect of its opposite matter. Internally, however, the Unit can have no experience except the witnessing of its own creations. Externally all is experience and the intense consciousness that results from friction and interdealing with other Units. One is free only as he recognizes that others are free, and this consciousness arises from encountering objective necessity. Out of this clash of pure forces is created the visible universe, operating in manifestation with mathematical exactitude and supported by invisible laws. Its energy is the energy of all. In it physical bodies are shields to intercept such waves of energy as their vibratory rate can encounter and modify. In it Units of Force realize the existence and experience the life of other Units of Force. Under our hypothesis there can be no other way. The unknowable may be felt in the heart as emotion or adoration, but the Lost Self for which the soul is constantly seeking is all the Universe which is not I.

5. Abnormal Aspects of Periodicity.

(a.) **Necessity.**

If one were asked what his heart most desires he probably would answer: "The eternal possibility of experience." If he only knew, there were no need of such a request, for in necessity the gift is already in his hands, however lightly he may at the time esteem it. By necessity we mean, first, the necessity for specialization of the Law as explained in the preceding paragraph, and, second, the mathematical principles in the combinations that make the environment of life. These countless tendencies inherent in the Law itself are the specializations of the Law, and each reveals a quality distinctively its own and desirable as a ground and possibility of a special experience. The intensity of individual experiences may vary, but the quality of the whole is inherent in each part. Little constellations and systems of motion may pattern after big, and size is only a dynamic distinction between all straight lines, circles, squares and other figures.

The first and simplest expression of the Law of Necessity is that Causes once set in operation create a rhythmic figure of motion closing at and passing through its initial point, and without outside interference, thus continuing forever. This form may be considered as either rest or motion, having in itself the full qualities of both elements. This being the case, it follows that each of us carries about with him his world of causation, already manifested, and standing back of him as a perpetual support to make him what he is. Indeed, he would be nothing at all without this internal gyroscope to give him a personal plane of motion that can and does run counter to every other plane.

When man sees within him this necessity and first feels its enormous potency and weight, it is liable to absorb his whole view. "There is naught without cause, there will be naught without cause and I stand nerveless and powerless realizing the force of this irresistible current and ready to resign myself to its over-whelming waves." The escape is not to realize less necessity and causation, but to experience its all embracing quality to the limit. Such an one is "Near the Kingdom," for all cause is no cause except as supported by a perpetual, inherent and constant fountain of creation which is the same will and desire that now battles with its former creations. Under our hypothesis, there is naught which man can experience, sense, or be conscious of—there is not the slightest event that can come in to lure or oppress him—that is not a matter in which he has already participated as a full and equal partner, or one which to interest him at all must be half supported by the manifested energy of himself as a Unit of Force. Let him learn once to call in and withdraw from general circulation this energy which he has given forth and he will see how quickly the mood and complexion of the whole matter will change. The pull, the stress, the strain, the whirl of every event which oppresses or overwhelms him is but the rhythmic motion of the energy which he himself has given forth. True, the form of motion is a resultant of the other forces he encountered, but he got as much as was taken and the scales of Justice hang even.

This habit and settled tendency of motion, or pure periodicity of manifested energy, is the only field of consciousness, and forms the visible world. It is the realm which science investigates and out of which she extracts all her laws. It is the frictionless fly-wheel of existence keeping in motion the orbs of life when they desire to gaze in the still mirror of the soul and by internal illumination behold its working. It is pure necessity, unsupported by any cause except its exact opposite, the free will or desire which gave it birth, but which is the same will that can work over and modify it in any particular, by paying the same price in energy as was originally paid for these imperishable goods. Evolution is "mathematics" plus "will," and the two are eternal life.

(b.) The Free Will.

As **something** by its very nature necessitates **nothing** or space, so **freedom** (the will) by its very nature implies restriction or necessity.

Freedom in its clash with itself, through divisibility or number, implies necessity.

As **one** will **alone** would be **no** will, and as will or freedom can be had only through the **many**, represented by things or other wills, this very many makes for restriction, which is called, for want of a better term, **necessity.**

This is the master parallel in opposition in energy itself—freedom and restriction.

Will as will (desire) is unconditioned, but as manifestation it is the reverse; so we have the conditioned, in its primitive attribute unconditioned, and the unconditioned in its expressions hedged about with conditions.

Back in primal consciousness man feels desire; this is intrinsic in his nature and wholly free and untrammelled. He may even have some special exterior object to which he directs it, but as long as he only desires, he is still free—his aspiration and longing being boundless; equal perhaps to his Unit of Force, and no other will can interfere. But let him once bring this unconditioned desire from the inner realm of freedom to the outer one of restrictions, where other once-free wills are fighting for supremacy, and he is environed immediately, and not only environed, but possibly prohibited in his attainment of that for which he longed.

Now one might argue that by the very fact that man

desires some **thing**, he conditions his will to the limit of that thing; but this is false reasoning, because will **is** desire of specials. Therefore, when he seeks them, the attribute is true to itself, which is freedom in desiring **something**—unlimited freedom in so doing.

We have written reverently of Force as the unthinkable source of energy, but para-force is purpose or desire; in fact, it seems to be an attribute in energy itself. Now we cannot write upon the subject of rhythm without touching upon this, and showing that while the law of periodicity is in no way changed by this other factor in energy, it may be, nevertheless, dealt with.

An energetic purpose may regulate rhythm without getting rid of it, and in the regulating carry out its aims in spite of it.

This freedom of will inwardly counts for **something** as much as does this restriction of will's expression outwardly.

This inward purpose, grace or aim, by its boundless interior freedom, comes forth into restricted environment, with the impetuosity of an engine, fired for an up-grade; and by its very speed and excess makes headway against inertia, and the impact of obstacles free like itself. To be sure its limitations are soon felt, but if the generator within is steady and hot with desire, it to an extent overrides difficulties somewhat as the locomotive leaps an unbridged chasm by its very impetus. We must not forget that while the limitations are forever there, that the freedom is there also, and the dilemma belongs, after all, to one principle.

Though a purposeful energy as energy may outwardly find its opposite in friction and inertia, if our hypothesis be true, that will and necessity are the master parallels in energy—what moral, ethical and practical use shall we make of this fact?

The Darwinian school of philosophers culminating in Spencer, while calling the will natural selection, nevertheless steer clear of the subject of freedom, and while not denying fail to emphasize it. On the other hand, in Germany was to be found one strenuous advocate of the world's will in the person of Schopenhauer. Each school strove to build a system for practical living upon its base.

But where is the Mencius of modern psychology, who not only recognizes polarity, but teaches its application in the golden mean of **living?**

It is easy to posit hypothetical principles and not altogether difficult to gather data to partially substantiate them, but when **ethics** are to flower out of the same it is quite another affair. Since the age of Greek philosophy, polarity or the identity of contraries has been harped upon and wrangled about, the Kantian school, especially, basing upon it; but if this principle be the key to balance and right adjustment, physically, mentally, psychically, why in the name of all that is great and modern has it not taught us the practical solution of the problems of life?

What do mental gymnasts amount to if they cannot apply their formulas and principles to the solving of the puzzle of life itself?

Though this work presents no new hypothesis, it does claim uniqueness in the emphasis of an old one—an emphasis so pronounced that it insists that from the law of rhythm may be deduced the fairest and best-advanced method of living in use in modern times.

In Ancient China Confucius built up and added to the antique "Book of Changes," crudely perhaps but nevertheless surely, by the law of rhythm alone foretelling and foreseeing results impossible of discovery otherwise.

Life was read in the classic days of Old Cathay by the law of periodicity, and possibly we moderns have somewhat yet to learn from that ancestral race.

CHAPTER X.

Poise.

Those who have read with atttenion the pages of the preceding chapters of this book will have observed that, while we have been true to our hypothesis that mind and matter are polarized aspects of the same thing, we have nevertheless enlarged the concept so as to speak with confidence of the Units of Force and their interdealing. This has been no random departure, nor artful device, but, as we intend it, a logical fruition of the original insight of our hypothesis.

The parallelism of mind and matter, as we have seen, is not because of any impossible gulf between the two, but for just the opposite reason. They are parallels by inner necessity and dependence. One cannot exist without the other. Each has its function to perform in supporting and explaining the other. They are opposite poles of the same process or thing.

This opposition between mind and matter is merely dynamic, a complete polarity and nothing more. It is idle to rank one above the other. It is futile to attempt to comprehend one without understanding the other. Indeed, the mission of this book is to show that in investigating one you are studying the other, that if you conquer one, you may rule the other. The laws of nature work in both realms, but in reverse application. Force is constant. Its contrary aspects of mind and matter are opposite poles of one thing.

Proceeding under our hypothesis, we have attempted to show that consciousness is a whole, having parts; that desire or will is the moving cause of all that exists; that action and reaction are equal; and that emotion accompanies the flow of all energy. We have taken up the problem of pleasure and pain and shown their necessary balance. We have studied imagery, memory and imagination, and intuition, and struggled with the understanding. In the last chapter we have faced the horned dilemma of periodicity and free will, and established the Master Parallel. But to what end is such an investigation unless through it we are to reach illumination and a Master's poise? We shall not speak of this final adjustment, this balance, this motion so rapid that it may seem rest, without curbing rhetorical expression, and again taking up the cold formula which must stand or fall as scientific fact.

The best expression of the completed hypothesis that results from the investigations of this book we think is found in the words of another. "**We postulate immortal Units of Force, each having the power to generate a constant but limited amount of energy, and no two alike in quantity.**" (Hatch, Scientific Occultism, p. 5.) It is our inevitable conclusion that the phenomena of mind and matter necessitate the postulate of a unit, and a unit not of matter, nor of mind, but of Force. We hold that each unit has the power to generate a constant but limited amount of energy, and that no two are alike in quantity. As to there being units, we expect little dissent. Their immortality we base on the nature of motion or rhythm itself. By the workings of this law, we find that consciousness parallels unconsciousness as its inseparable mate, and that the Law of Rhythm conditions both and becomes our foundation. The power to generate energy is for us a mystery, apparently an insoluble fact. We recognize it reverently, forced to subjectivity in its contemplation. The remaining and crucial point of the hypothesis is that each Unit of Force is limited in its amount of energy, and that no two are alike in quantity.

If this be provable at all, it will be by a statement so simple that its power may easily be overlooked, or by an experience so profound that few can reach it. We shall not struggle in argumentation regarding the point, knowing that each reader will fix his own attitude, and, if hostile, will seek diligently to find an exception to this curious law.

The power to generate energy is but the power to maintain motion at some rate. If the rate of motion is fixed, the amount of energy is limited, although its intensity may vary. Frequency, amplitude, and wave length are special and relative aspects of the original vibratory capacity. It is the number of combinations possible with other vibrations that determines the result. This being the case, our postulate of Units, limited in their power to generate energy, simply means that they can make only certain combinations with other units. This is illustrated perfectly by the prime numbers of mathematics. Indeed, it is more than an illustration, for we think the external world is made of mathematics—but of mathematics ensouled and rightly understood. In number we find exactly the fixed and solvent quality necessary for a living thing, a perfect symbol of the One and the many of all philosophic systems.

In polarity we find the key to all manifested energy, its rhythmic motions being computable and in their certainty forming a stable element in all the flux and change, which otherwise would baffle us and make impossible a rational system. But polarity, as we conceive it, is grounded in a subtler and deeper principle. For want of a better name, we call it will or desire. What we desire to know is whether or not will is a fact. Finding it everywhere, as the other half of mathematics or necessity, we assign to it equal validity and proclaim its existence without apology or hesitation. We also accept the consequences of responsibility that flow from it. But the beginning of will under our hypothesis is so simple that we often overlook it to turn to its more complicated manifestations. At the bottom it is the power to act or not, as one wants. If there is no activity or motion, there is no energy. If there is no energy generated, the Unit is free.

The power to act or not to act at will, residing in the Unit of Force, is in the finality a pure polarity. It is a push or a pull that may be exerted at any time, or in any direction. In stricter analysis, we see that it manifests in a consciousness which may be so polarized as to transcend all except the rhythmic aspects of space and time. This freedom and potency may produce tremendous results.

In acting or not acting, one has full control over the setting in motion of new causes. Through the subtler aspects of the principle of polarity, the point of contact or injection of a new cause in the external world may be determined. The quantity of energy manifested may also be controlled. In this way the consequences of one's act may be gauged in advance. Causes already in operation may likewise be modified to any extent by paying the necessary price in energy to redeem them from objective slavery.

In withdrawing energy from the objective world there is nothing lost. We do not toy with the idea of something from nothing and nothing replacing something. Our philosophy is too energized to countenance such an illusion. What disappears as motion must reappear as mass. The insulation of polarity makes this possible, and conserves perfectly the energy which otherwise would be without explanation. Mass would seem to be internal motion capable of acting externally upon breaking through its proper insulation. Assuming a cause to be operating in the external world, if any Unit of Force pays the price in energy necessary to relieve himself from responsibility, he in the act restores to the others energy sufficient to make the modified cause carry the same mass. In this way the equation of energy is maintained.

In this way, using our original hypothesis, we have come to the conclusion that the amount of energy of the unit is constant. By this we mean that in manifestation it is always an equation, action and reaction being equal. Measured by rhythm, each term works with mathematical exactitude. It is a theory of absolute offset or deferred balance. Action being equal to reaction, there is in one sense neither time nor motion in the event, except as maintained by polarity or the shifting of the pole of consciousness of the Unit of Force. To maintain this theory, the rule must be logically stated, and the various apparent exceptions explained.

We first call attention to the fact that all bodies seem dominated by an internal consciousness or force. It is also true that there is a limit to the force exerted. The amount of matter which we see held together in complexly organized bodies is not large, and the rule would seem to place a limit upon all forms of organization held together by a unitary force. Externally, there is no unit visible. Mass simply appears and theoretically may increase without limit, or be infinitely divisible. We conclude, therefore, that the Unit of Force appears as a unit only internally, and recognizes its own limitations. In the same manner it establishes its force lines and determines the center of gravity of its interests.

This being the case, the Unit of Force in dealing with any rhythm or cycle of manifested energy, can generate or maintain a limited though constant amount of energy determinable by the mathematical combinations possible between the normal vibration rate of the Unit of Force and the dominant note of the evolutionary cycle in which it appears. In other words, the unit can generate a constant but limited amount of energy, or vibratory activity, and in all its interdealings with the Units of Force so manifesting, will be limited to the amount of energy at any time at its disposal. This may vary greatly, as the Unit may conserve its energy and the resulting mass will carry the potentiality of the whole.

Taking man as an exemplification of the working of this law, we find that he has infancy, manhood and old age. He is weak as a child and at old age again closes the rhythm with helplessness. By our hypothesis, his energy in childhood is absorbed in elaborating the growing tissues and pushing forward to efficient adult strength. In the prime of manhood the most energy is available and little is needed to preserve the body in harmonious action. It is free to work in a thousand ways. Many processes formerly requiring conscious effort have now been reduced to automatic processes. The energy used in aquiring a thousand habits and in active sense perception and contacting the external world, may now be used for mental processes that involve judgment, deliberation and purposeful dealing with men. In old age this free energy is again drawn in. Finding the accretions of old age dimming his experiences, man loses interest in the body and prepares for departure. Various activities have absorbed and used up his whole energy. Until freed by rejuvenation or death he cannot progress.

The same rule is applicable to food and nourishment. Food and drink is first taken with avidity, a keen appetite making eating one of the pleasures of life. The well-regulated body, however, knows the limit of its energy and indicates the time when partaking of food must cease. The energy used in digesting and elaborating food as nourishment of the body is equal in amount to the sustenance and energy derived therefrom. Although the processes of metabolism and katabolism are not exactly simultaneous, the balance must at some time be struck. The energy which the body acquires through food is not the energy of the Unit of Force which dominates the body. Food energy is the energy of forces which the dominant unit guides and controls. The life force of any body is merely force consciously applied at critical points, to regulate and repair. Other forces within the body work automatically, and are not life forces except for themselves. There is no conscious force except that of the Unit of Force. All else is alien matter, and no more a part of man's complete body than his clothing, the house in which he lives and the moving air. The quantity of food the body can assimilate depends upon the amount of co-operating units and elements the Unit of Force maintains. The energy which the Unit can manifest or release depends on how well he has regulated and laid out his plans. Inasmuch, however, as manifestation of energy to him is nothing except as it awakens consciousness, he limits himself to maintaining senses active and keen, and motion sufficient to give them a variety of experiences.

With reference to stimulants and narcotics, it must be that the temporary exhilaration or pleasurable feeling (through a release of energy resulting in consciousness) is always balanced by the effort and pain of repairing the damage.

A weak man loses his grip and pulls himself together. In this he applies his energy to co-ordinate and repair. Harmonious action is repeated rhythmically until diverted by internal forces.

Emotion is enervating because it is energy applied externally and lodged in cause and effect until reaction has returned it to its source.

Anger breaks out because man charges his body with energy tending toward certain things, and it may require a serious expenditure of new energy to repair the damage.

Music conquers chaos because it sets a harmonic pattern with which the body is already in sympathy, and may readily copy.

We shall not attempt to give further illustrations of the manifold equations of energy, and may well leave this fruitful field to others. The poise of which this chapter speaks is but the recognition of the reality of such equilibrated forces and the preserving of approximate balance. It is realizing the value of energy too precious to be wasted, for it purchases all there is. This understanding can result only from experience. It is the wares brought home by the rich freighter which has sailed the stormy seas of many lives. It is a breaking of force lines which brings together by a new path diverse things, so that the memory thereby escapes its bondage to the chain of events, and sees primal causes and effects. It is a short cut between things you are interested in, rearranging the pattern of the beads spun by the loom of time. Through it we behold Units of Force, the whole in quality, conditioning all the universe which is not we—but He is not a perfect God without us.

If one watches an acrobat walking a tight rope, he will get some idea of the finesse of balance, a poise conditioned on one central thought, that of maintaining a position essential to walking the rope. But to keep this possibility valid, a multiplicity of attitudes must be assumed, any attitude that prevents falling and helps toward the ultimate aim. It is the much mooted law of the one and the many, and the many and the one over and over again; one purpose, a single straightforward idea, maintained by an intricate and surprising variety of conditions necessary to its preservation. The athlete on the tight rope leans this way and that. If not expert, he bows and bends, plunges forward, throws himself back, extends his arms, elevates and drops them, the nicest quantity of weight ever in his mind; his movements automatic rather than conscious, for he thinks only of one thing, the maintenance of his balance in crossing this perilous bridge. Man, in spanning the chasm between birth and death, walks a fearfully narrow path. Gravitation pulls him toward the abyss below, a thousand things—the sky, the stars, the almost ravishing beauty of his environment—line his eyes and mind from the chief idea, that of maintaining himself balanced between attraction and repulsion, an individual still, neither overwhelmed by the spell of gravity nor the charm of beauty. To poise is the art of the mental athlete. He may be young and the path new; perhaps he will bend and writhe and distort himself in order to hold his own and keep true to his aim. Dignity in the exacting struggle has not yet arrived, but practice in time will make of him a sublime figure, beautifully poised, with but slight outer indication of the dangers assailing him. Erect, sraightforward, clean cut, he will march to the goal beyond, upheld by the law of rhythmic balance, happy in his supremacy over difficulties, complete and absolute in his majesty of will.